How to Become an Overachiever

David E. Carter

How to Become an Overachiever

ISBN: 1-892350-00-9

Published by
London Books, Ltd.
4100 Executive Park Drive, #16
Cincinnati, OH 45241

(513) 421-1938

How to Become an Overachiever

**This book is dedicated to Christa and Lauren.
May you make the most out of your opportunities.**

What is an Overachiever?

An overachiever is someone who:

1. was once thought to be very "average," with little chance of significant success . . . who then
2. made personal changes and became a highly successful individual.

Profile of overachievers

• **Education** — Almost 50% have college degrees. But more than half did *not* complete college. Many overachievers did not attend college at all.

• **Age** — There's no age limit. Some people make the necessary changes at 19. Others have become overachievers after retirement!

• **Sex** — Most are men. But a growing number of women are becoming overachievers.

• **Geographic area** — Overachievers are everywhere — in small towns as well as big cities. And they're all over the world.

• **Work background** — Many were people who had "settled" for a low-level job before discovering the potential they had within. Others were executives — victims of corporate America's"downsizing" — who discovered that losing their jobs meant opportunity, not disaster.

One common trait among overachievers:

they *change* the things that are holding them back;

they take *action* to remove the barriers to their success.

Note: Being an overachiever is not the same as being a workaholic. In fact, many overachievers have more leisure time than people who work a 40-hour week in "regular" jobs.

Preface

I've spent a lot of my adult life in the company of many highly successful people. I've spent even more time around people who are, by all measures, "average."

The "average" people would be surprised to know that there's *very little difference* between the people who achieve high levels of success and those who don't.

I did a little research on "success" and found out some very encouraging facts.

Highly successful people often are no smarter than average. Try on this fact: High school valedictorians, as a group, have *no* greater chance of achieving success than the "average" students who don't get to sit on the stage at graduation.[1] In the research group studied, 75% of the valedictorians excelled in college, but once they joined the work force — in *real life* — most recorded only average achievements. (That's a pretty encouraging piece of information, unless you happen to be a valedictorian.) Here's another fact which will warm the hearts of under-achieving students everywhere: a study of the MBA class of 1974 at the Harvard Business School indicates that those who scored *lowest* on standardized admissions tests are making the most money today.[2]

Most people have far more potential ability than they ever realize. The "10 steps to becoming an overachiever" in this book are based on observations I have made of many highly successful people. Early in this book, you will meet seven "average" people. Then, you will follow their stories, chapter by chapter, as they make the changes needed to become overachievers.

[1]For you footnote fans, this fact came from a study done by Karen Arnold and Terry Denny, professors in the education department at Boston College.

[2]This information came from a really interesting book — *The New Rules* — by Prof. John P. Kotter of the Harvard Business School. If you're serious about becoming an overachiever, buy *his* book too.

If you *really* want to make the most of your abilities,

this book will tell you how to do it.

You may remember the "bell-shaped curve" from some of your classes in school.

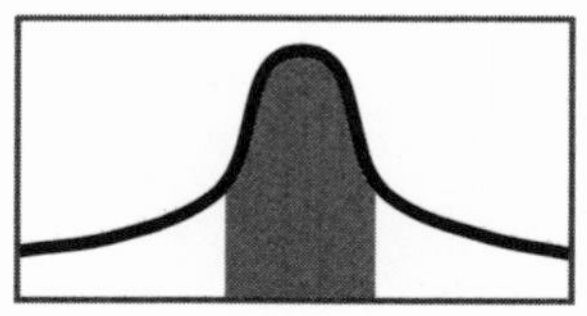

The gray area in the middle is "average." Most people fall into this range.

The object of this book is to show you the way to stop being "average" and how to move into the far right end of the chart that is reserved for overachievers.

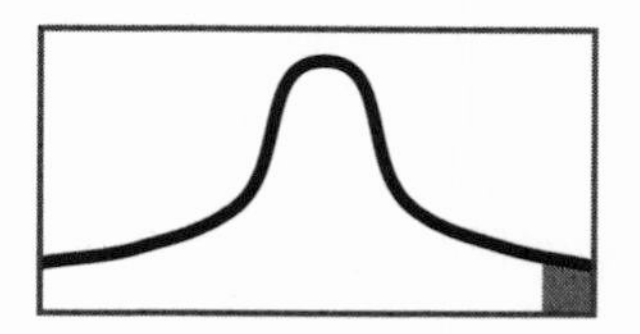

The small grey gray area to the right is where you'll

find the overachievers. Not many people get there.

But, before you're through reading this book,you're going to

see just how *easy* it is to attain success.

"Permanent Record"

To many people, the phrase "Permanent Record" immediately opens a dark memory of a stern teacher pointing a finger and saying *"this will be on your Permanent Record."* Those words still bring a chill to many otherwise well-adjusted adults.

Every time I got a bad grade on a report card, (in high school, that was a pretty common event), I was certain that my Permanent Record was being further stained. I began to believe that my chances for future success were nonexistent — due to the Permanent Record which the teachers said would "follow me forever."

The reality is that huge numbers of highly successful people were pretty average for a large part of their life — and their Permanent Records were often less than desirable. Following is a list of the people you'll meet in this book.[1] For each, there are negative comments which might have appeared on their "permanent record" early in life. This is followed by a brief description of their life's accomplishments — after they became overachievers.

These seven stories will be an inspiration to anyone

who wants to better himself or herself.

[1]The names of most of the people have been changed. However, Teresa Wright said "I want my real name in the book. It'll be good for business." And, of course, my name is real, since I want people who watched my loaf through high school to see my name on the cover and wonder "is that really the David Carter that I used to know?"

Permanent Records which will inspire you

Jim Harris

Permanent Record: Average student in high school. "Below average" student in 3 1/2 years of college. Actually, Jim showed signs of brilliance — when he was in class. But after he spent most of one semester living in the dorm at a *different* university 60 miles away, his "real college" suggested it was best if he didn't return. Suddenly an ex-student, he was quickly fired from a grocery store clerk's job because he "made too many jokes with the customers." At age 22, he was working part-time in a men's store.

Today: As one of Hollywood's highest-regarded TV writer-producers, he currently is involved in writing, producing or consulting on three prime time network shows — all in the top 12 in the Nielsen rating, and he is currently writing the pilot for a fourth. He was also a writer for *The Tonight Show Starring Johnny Carson* for a total of 13 years, and was the only writer to work for Carson in all four decades of his reign. He was the only writer to be asked to stay on when Jay Leno took over the show. He has won most every award possible for a TV writer.

Brad Thomas

Permanent Record: Average student in high school. Dropped out of college at age 19 to start a business cleaning 18-wheel trucks with a high-pressure water hose. He borrowed $2,500 to buy a used bread truck (his grandfather had to co-sign the note). In the early years, of the small business. Brad's future looked bleak. At one point, he was 3 months behind on his truck payment, and was within 30 days of having it (and his dream) repossessed.

Today: Five years ago, Brad sold his company for $23 million. Today, at age 44, he oversees a division of a Fortune 500 firm with annual sales in excess of $200 million. Brad also owns a shirt factory and has various other financial interests. Although he still keeps busy with business, he has time to enjoy his accomplishments; one of his favorite activities is flying one of his fleet of restored antique airplanes.

Mal Charles

Permanent Record: Fairly good student in high school, although he never took books home. He got a job in a steel mill shortly after high school, and was able to get a two-year technical degree while he worked the midnight shift. However, when the steel industry went into a decline, he was laid off for two years. He and his wife had a small child, and they had just moved into a new house with a big mortgage. Suddenly jobless, he had no marketable skills, and his family was facing a very uncertain future.

Today: He once owned a successful retail store in a large regional mall, but discovered that he could be more profitable by concentrating on the wholesale customers — not retail. He recently changed locations and is building a national clientele of custom embroidered apparel.

David Warren

Permanent Record: David remembers his high school years very well. " I was a Truant Officer's Nightmare," he says with a smile. He spent most of his sophomore year of high school cutting class, (over 80 absences) and failed two subjects. In his high school class of about 1,000 people, he graduated "maybe 997 or 998. There had to be 2 or 3 people who were below me." He couldn't get into a "good" college, and had to literally "beg" the admissions officer to get into a 2-year college.

Today: Nationally known physical therapist who has taught his techniques for preventing back injury to thousands of people. He also owns a growing chain of physical therapy clinics.

Randy Carniak

Permanent Record: Average student in high school; his main interests were girls and sports. "After those things, I just didn't have time for books." After two years in college, his record was OK, but was nothing to brag about. As a junior and senior, he was an excellent student, but after graduating, he couldn't find a "good" job for about a year. During the long search for employment, he cut grass and painted houses. "At age 23, I was the best educated house painter in town," he says.

Today: Although he's barely 35, he's national sales manager for his firm — with 14 people reporting to him. (And he's never been a field salesman.) He has major profit responsibility for a large division of his employer — a nationally-known clothing company. He works directly with the president of the firm.

Theresa Wright

Permanent Record: Graduated from a small rural high school; named "most likely to succeed" by classmates. Although she had 16 college credits when most of her classmates were just starting university classes, she took a job instead of going on to school. A few months later, in front of her office building, she was abducted and traumatized by a gunman. Soon thereafter, she married "to have a protector." When the relationship ended, she and her infant daughter went back to her small home town of less than 1,000 people, where she stayed for 5 years. As a single mother with no real job skills, living in a very small town, her future looked bleak.

Today: Real estate sales Superstar. (Note the capital S in Superstar. She deserves it.) She's constantly among Century 21's "Top 100" producers nationally, and her annual income puts her in the upper 1% of all Americans.

David Carter

(That's me — the name on the cover of this book.) ***Permanent Record:*** In 9th grade my math teacher told me "you're not college material." Unfortunately, I believed her and graduated in the lower half of my high school class. Nearly flunked out of college in freshman year.

Today: Graduate of University of Kentucky School of Journalism; master's degree in advertising from Ohio University; MBA from Syracuse University. Graduate of the Harvard Business School's 3-year program for company presidents. Founder of twelve businesses; still own seven. I've made more than 20 trips to Asia to conduct seminars and to act as a consultant for some large, global companies based in Indonesia and Thailand. Author of more than 70 books about advertising and corporate logos; these books are published by two major firms and are distributed all over the world. (And, of course, I wrote this book.)[1] My 9th grade teacher was wrong.

Obviously, having a negative "Permanent Record" is no barrier to success.

If you *really* want to be an overachiever,

you can do it.

The Ten Steps in Becoming an Overachiever

1. **Discover why success is so easy.**
2. **Decide to change.**
3. **Dream — Then set some goals.**
4. **Start Listening. People will tell you how to succeed.**
5. **Take action!**
6. **Learn to "steal time."**
7. **Promote Yourself**
8. **Look for ways to "double promote" yourself.**
9. **Multiply.**
10. **Keep it up.**

You will notice that all ten of these steps include an *action* word.

No matter how much you "want" success, without *action*, it's not going to happen.

[1] If you're just browsing in the book store and are reading this, now would be an appropriate time to take this to the cashier, buy the book, take it home and really start reading it while sitting down.

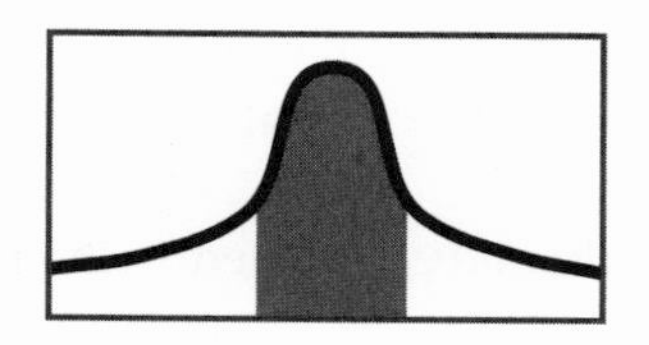

1. Discover why success is so easy.

The overwhelming majority of people have a winner inside them — just waiting to be let out. But the sad fact is — that *potential* ability for major success is *never* awakened in most people.

Successful people often talk about how easy it was to "make it." The truth is that success is so easy because most people *never even try* to raise above "average." (A lot of people who *could* compete with you for success will never even try.)

For every hundred people who have an idea or opportunity which will propel them upward, only a small percent ever take the action necessary to move them from being "ordinary" into "someone who really get things done."

Take this test.

I was recently asked to give a talk to a group of already-successful business people who were in the Executive MBA program at Syracuse University. Here's how I opened my speech:

> You wouldn't be here if you didn't want to better yourself. But let me ask you a single question. Have you ever had an idea — say for a new product, or a new business — and then a year or so later, saw a magazine article or an ad with that same idea?

Nearly everyone in the room held up a hand. Almost all of these people once had an idea — which *someone else* acted upon — that could have made them highly successful. But not one of them had ever taken the *action* step — the one thing you must do in order to become *really* successful.

I repeat: **Success is so easy because most people *never even try* to raise above "average."**

The field isn't exactly crowded with competitors.

Instead, most people are content to sit on the sidelines and be spectators, while the people who choose to take part in the competition reap the rewards (financial and emotional) that come with success.

Those who do decide to enter life's "fast lane" will discover that the road to success is a 6-lane highway with light traffic. The road that's *really* crowded is the one-way, dead-end street.

Why people don't try.

I have talked with many people who had ideas for starting a business or for really moving up the corporate ladder and encouraged them to "go for it." I'm amazed at the many reasons people can come up with for not even trying to accomplish more. Here are the most common excuses:

1. What if I fail?

2. I live in a big city. (Or — I'm in a huge company) There's no way I can compete with all the smart people here.

3. I live in a small town. (Or — I work for a small company.) There's no way I can be a big success here.
4. What'll my friends say? (What will my co-workers say?) They'll think I'm trying to be better than them.

5. I could never do something like *that*. (Translation: I'm afraid of leaving my "comfort zone.")

There's not a good *reason* in all those responses. They're all *excuses*.

Here's my response to those excuses.

What if I fail? By trying, you have at least *some* chance of success. **Not even trying is a 100% guarantee that you will not succeed.** And if you *do* fail, so what?

Failure is not a permanent condition;
it is a learning experience, in which you discover
what *not* to do the next time.

Smart people learn from their failures, and use that knowledge to improve future results. All the people in this book had some kind of failure to overcome — and they all did it. Don't fear failure — learn from it. And grow stronger from the experience.

I live in a big city. (I'm in a big company.) What better place to be? If you're in a big city or firm, that means there are a lot of successful businesses (and business people) you can look to for guidance. Role models for your success are everywhere. The large population or the large business means that big opportunities are there.

I live in a small town. (I'm in a small company.) This is the worst *excuse* of all. Small towns and small firms are a great place to succeed. Important relationships, such as banking, are much easier to establish in a small town than in a big city. Networking is much easier when you live in a small town. And in a small town or small firm, you can get to know top people really well. You can see first-hand how a small company is run. The greatest opportunities for people today are in starting small companies.

About the "small town" syndrome: A lot of people who don't live in a huge city seem to have an inferiority complex about their geographic status. People who use the "small town" excuse should carefully read the next paragraph. Better still, copy it and put it where you'll see it every day.

[1] All the overachievers in this book are from one town of less then 30,000 population.

There is no monopoly on brains and bright ideas — where I.Q. is rationed out only to people who live in a big city or in a certain part of the country.[1]

What'll my friends say? So — are you willing to sacrifice your future just because your friends and co-workers don't share your desire to achieve something? Are you going to let your ambition and potential go to waste just because some of your friends don't share your goals?

Are you willing to abandon your dreams just because your friends aren't as ambitious as you are?

Fear of leaving the "comfort zone."

Literally *millions* of potential overachievers with a *huge* aptitude for success stay on the sidelines as "spectators" because they're afraid to leave their personal "comfort zone." This fear translates into an negative attitude which says "I can't do that."

Whether you think "I can do that," or "I can't do that," you're right.

Fear of leaving the comfort zone: a case study

I want to illustrate just how powerful the "comfort zone fear" is with an example of someone I've known for a long time. John W. had only a high school education, but he was bright and a hard worker. After serving in the Air Force for three years, he got an office job at an industrial plant. He started as a clerk, but quickly was given more responsibility. Soon, he was supervising three other clerks. He learned quickly, and had the ability to quickly analyze business situations and make appropriate decisions on the spot. He caught the attention of the plant manager, who sent him on an important assignment to visit the home office in Los Angeles. During his week on the west coast, he also impressed a number of executives at headquarters. When he returned home, he was given a major opportunity: he was invited to become a part of the plant management team, as supervisor of the entire office staff. Thirty-seven people would work under him.

John thought about the offer over a weekend. On Monday, he went to his boss, and asked, "If I take this job, will I have to leave the union?"

"Yes, of course," the boss said. "You'll be a part of management. And this will just be the start for you. You're young, and you can go a long way in this company. You have the potential to have my job someday ... maybe even more."

"But if I leave the union, you can fire me any time you want to," he said sadly. "If I stay in the union, I'll have a job as long as the plant operates." He took a deep breath and paused before saying, "I just can't give up the security of the union job. What if I don't get the job done — then I'm gone and I can't get my old job back." That's how the discussion ended.

John had enormous potential. But his fear of leaving his personal comfort zone kept him from making a change. He looked at opportunity and saw only risk. He wasn't able to see a little further and discover the huge opportunities that were waiting out there for him.

Most people will stay in their personal comfort zone, because they look past their current situation and see only risk. They fail to look beyond the uncertainty to see the many opportunities which lie ahead.

Just like the people you'll read about in this book, you have a huge amount of potential inside you. Don't be like John W., and let all that potential die. Don't be afraid to leave your personal comfort zone.

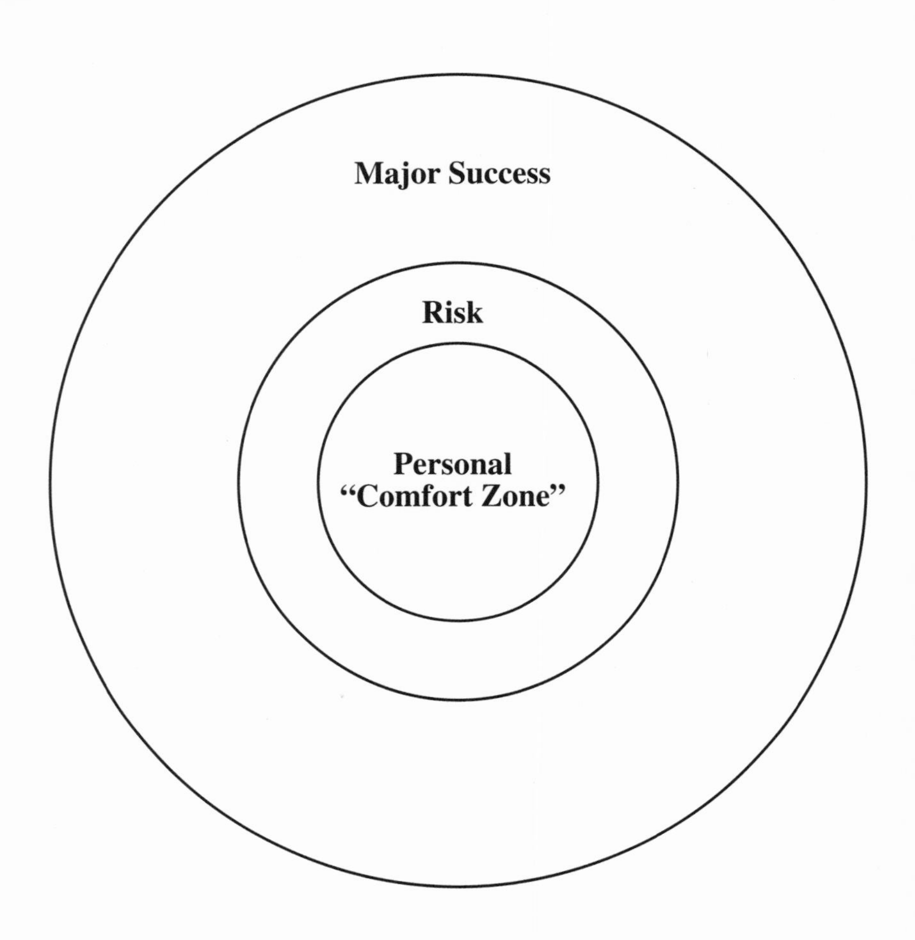

The road to success involves going through risk.

As long as you stay in your “comfort zone,” you’ll never achieve any great degree of success.

You now have two choices: You can discover the 10 steps outlined in this book and really get on the road to becoming an overachiever. Or you can follow the path of most people, and stay in your comfort zone, with no chance of ever finding the successful person who is inside you — the one just waiting to get out.

John W. — 25 years later.

Just a quick follow up on John's career. Since he made it clear to management that he didn't want to leave the protection of the union, they didn't spend any more time in grooming him for a better position. He retired at age 62, still in the union, but unhappy in his dead-end job.

He occasionally speaks about people he trained — who later went into management positions. Two of them became plant managers. In his reflective moments, he says, "I could have done that. I was given the chance. I was smart enough... but ....." He doesn't have a way to end the sentence. The truth is, he *could* have done it. He *was* given the chance. And he *was* smart enough. But he didn't do anything about it. He was never able to leave his personal comfort zone.

> You probably know people like John. Have **you** ever turned down opportunity because you feared leaving your comfort zone? What were you really afraid of?

What are you going to do with *your* life?

Are you content to stay in your comfort zone? Or will you take a small risk in order to possibly achieve more than you ever dreamed possible?

> **The future belongs to the risk takers.**

Vast numbers of people with a lot of ability will never try anything new — they won't venture outside their "comfort zone." Most people are so caught up in the process of "making a living" that they never really attempt to become successful. They get so caught up in their day-to-day existence that they don't ever ask "how good can I be?" It never occurs to them that they can set their goals a little higher — or a *lot* higher — and quite possibly reach them.

Most people *let* things happen;
overachievers *make* things happen.

What is success?

Since this is a "success" book, I thought it would be a good idea if I came up with a definition of success. After searching for just the right definition for months, I heard these words of wisdom at a university graduation address recently:

Success is the freedom to choose your own destiny.

Success is the ability to face life — on your terms.

Being Successful means getting up in the morning and looking forward to the day.

Notice that these definitions of success don't mention money. An interesting point made by several people in this book is that you don't become a successful person by chasing money; money *follows* successful people. Find something you like — do it very well — and you'll become successful.

Why *you* are different

Just by buying this book, you have already shown that you have the desire to better yourself. As you read this book, you're going to meet several role models — "average" people who found the power within themselves to change and become very **un**-average.

Unfortunately, for most people, it's much easier just to get a job, collect a paycheck, and not take any risks. But when people live their lives like that, the huge potential inside them will never be found. Sometimes, though, all it takes is just a gentle push from an outsider to make people *see* their potential — and start overachieving.

"Come to the edge," he said.

They said: "We are afraid."

"Come to the edge," he said.

They came.

He pushed them...

and they flew.

The goal of this book is to give you a gentle push.

Now — get ready to *fly.*

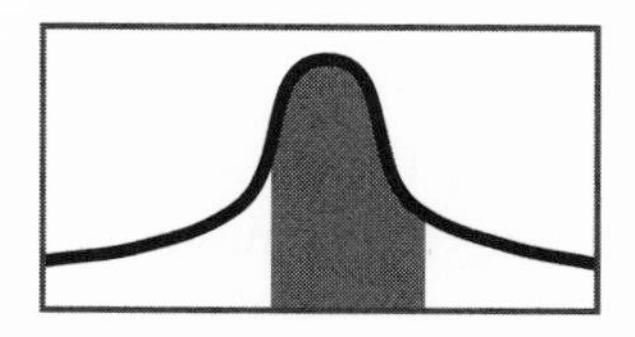

2. Decide to change.

Almost all overachievers have a similar history: at some point in their adult life, each was thought of as being "average," with no particular potential for achieving major success. Then, somehow, they all *changed.* They changed their attitudes, changed their goals, changed their work habits — and eventually they changed their lives.

If you really want to become better than you are, the first step comes when you *decide to change.*

Jim Harris

At age 22, Jim Harris was not exactly on life's "fast track." He had been a lackluster student in high school. He didn't even buy books his senior year. His high school guidance counselor once burst into tears when she found out he had an IQ of over 150. He was not a particularly motivated student when he moved on to his hometown community college, but he completed two years with average grades. His real downfall came when he went away to a university.

Jim remembers those days well. "I was at Denison University, which was an easy drive from the big school — Ohio State University. In the early fall, I went to OSU to spend the weekend visiting a friend. I had so much fun, I decided to stay. There was a vacant room in the dorm, so I just moved in. Of course, I wasn't attending my classes back at Denison, but I was meeting a lot of people at Ohio State, and learning a lot from going to some classes there. (Only my friend knew I wasn't registered.) I was so involved with stuff on the Ohio State campus that I was elected to the dorm council. I was particularly pleased when a paper about Thomas Hardy I ghosted for another student won a campus literary prize.

"I took part in a lot of dorm 'bull sessions,' discussing the issues of the day. At that time, politics was my first love. People thought I was a pretty bright student. They didn't know I was supposed to be in class *somewhere else* — at Denison. The semester I spent at Ohio State was very stimulating ... it's unfortunate that it doesn't appear on a transcript.

"In 1968, I skipped my state and local government mid-term at Denison and hitchhiked to Nebraska to volunteer for Bobby Kennedy's campaign. Of course, I flunked the class, but I learned a lot more about the political process from working in that primary than I would have memorizing meaningless facts for a test.

"When I finally returned to Denison I had an honest heart-to-heart talk with my advisor. He asked me what I 'really' wanted to do after college. I told him Johnny Carson was my hero and I would like to work for him. He laughed and told me to get my head out of the clouds and get back to work. 'Dreams were one thing; insanity was something else,' he said. I stood, shook his hand, thanked him for his time and as nicely as I could, told him he was a very intelligent and accomplished man; he could tell me a lot of things — but telling me what *my* dreams were was not one of them. I withdrew from all of my classes at Denison and took six incompletes. I walked off campus in April 1968, went home, and I gave myself a year to accomplish my goal.

"I would watch the Johnny Carson Show every night, and began to believe that I was just as funny as the writers who produced the jokes for the monologue. No, I *knew* I was just as talented as they were. Somewhere, I had read about the daily routine of comedy writers, and I began to create jokes for the Carson show every day. I would read the papers, pick topics, and then write material for the show. I didn't like doing homework for college, but I committed myself to writing comedy several hours every day. I treated it like my job, even though nobody saw what I was writing. By then, I was very confident that my ideas were just as good as the jokes on the show. I decided then that I *was* going to write for the Carson Show someday. But first, I changed my work habits."

Jim took a hard look at himself. Although he had hated to read articles and then write papers for school, he committed himself to reading several newspapers and magazines each day, then spending 4-5 hours writing funny material. Jim made a decision to change the things that were keeping him from being successful. He committed himself to developing work habits that he had never had before.

What things are keeping **you** from being successful? Are you willing to change?

David Warren

David Warren didn't like high school. "I was in Classical High, a college prep school in Springfield, Massachusetts and we had 6 class periods each day. In my sophomore year, I really hated my 5th & 6th period classes, so I just skipped most afternoons. After I had about 80 absences, the truant officer came to my house. I was there alone, but didn't answer the door. The guy slid a pretty stern letter under the door, but I just read it and threw it away. Needless to say, I failed those two classes and had to go to summer school to make it up. The main thing I learned that summer was *not* to fail a class, because summer school wasn't much fun. In the fall, I started going to all my classes, but didn't do a whole lot better with my grades. At least, I did enough work to avoid failing. My main goal in school was to avoid going to summer school again. Back then, grades weren't important to me, because I was convinced I was going to play baseball for the Boston Red Sox.

"When I graduated from high school, if there were a thousand people in my class, I must have finished about 997 or 998. I'm sure there were two or three people who had worse grades than I did, but I was very much on the bottom of the heap. I had barely made it through a college preparatory school, and I had no ambition to go on to college. None.

"After I finished high school, I had to figure out what I wanted to do with my life. It was pretty clear that the Red Sox weren't going to sign me, so my first thought was about being a coach or a teacher. But there weren't a lot of job openings in that field back then, so I thought about physical therapy. My grades were too low to get into a really competitive university, so I applied to a two-year school — Springfield Technical College — in 1970, and I had to *beg* my way in. The dean of admissions — a nice guy named Dr. Parkinson — simply told me that I couldn't make it academically there. I asked him for one chance.

I knew I wasn't an idiot. I *knew* I could do the work. But I also knew I had to *change*. When Dr. Parkinson gave me a provisional admission to the college, that was all I needed. I decided to become someone else, because now, everything counted. This was my *future*.

> What kind of future do you want? What changes do you need to make in order to obtain that future?

Theresa Wright

When Teresa Wright graduated from a small high school in a rural community, she was voted "Most Likely to Succeed" by her classmates. And by the time her college-bound classmates began their first classes in September 1974, she had already accumulated 16 credits — enough to be halfway through her freshman year. But Teresa wasn't in college then. She was working.

"When I was a little girl growing up in my small town, I used to be enthralled by the lights and smell of the city. When my parents would drive me to the big city nearest my home, I always dreamed of growing up and working there someday. Just after graduation, I went to the city to visit relatives, and was looking forward to finding a job there. After a few weeks of job hunting, though, I got homesick. At that exact time, the local bank president back home called and offered me a job . I agreed to take the job, but as soon as I'd done that, I knew I'd made a mistake. The next morning, I applied for a job at the largest employer in the city (a Fortune 100 company), and they called me to work the next day. I knew I'd be happier in the city. I was excited about my future.

"Just a few months later, something happened that was a major turning point in my life. I was taking some papers to another office downtown when a man jumped into my car and abducted me at gun point. After I drove him several miles, I was able to pull over and escape. But as I got out, he hit me in the head with his gun and I wound up in the hospital. I was just 19 years old, and was very proud to be living on my own, so I didn't want my parents to know about what had happened. They heard about it from a friend of mine back home who had seen the story on the evening newscast.

"Even though the incident was over, it still haunted me for a long time. My employer arranged for psychiatric help for me, which was very humiliating. At the depth of all this, I prayed for strength so that this problem wouldn't defeat me. The police had arrested the man, so I would have to testify at his trial, which was scheduled for late September. Then I began to get letters — threatening me if I testified. The pressure on me was so great. Just before the trial, I got married to a man I had met a few months before. Not because I loved him, but because I felt I needed a protector. I was married for three years and had a daughter. Once the marriage ended, my daughter and I went back home to my small town, and we stayed there for five years. For the entire time, I wanted out. I knew that the future had a lot to offer me, but only if I made some major changes in my life. When I was 28,

"I decided to take a real estate course, and began studying the books every spare moment I had. I knew that as soon as I passed the real estate exam, I could go back to the city — on my terms."

> How many single mothers would have simply said "this is what my life is going to be; I have no future" and stayed there forever? Too many people "settle" for less than they're capable of attaining. Are you settling for less than your potential? Are you ready to make the changes needed to improve your life?

Mal Charles

"I did OK in high school, but never took a book home. I was in a business course, not college prep, so it wasn't all that challenging. Just after I graduated, I got a summer job at the big steel mill close to home. That was in 1975. The economy was pretty strong, and at the end of summer, I was able to move up to a full-time job at the mill. For the first couple of years, I didn't work every day, since my seniority was so low. And when I did work, it was on midnight shift. I decided to use that schedule to my personal advantage, so I began attending Shawnee State College. I took electro-mechanical engineering. I finished the associate degree program, and as my seniority situation got better, I was working more regularly in the plant's shear department. When an opening for a clerical job came, I took it. The pay was less, but there was not much chance of a layoff. Or at least I thought so.

"When the recession hit the U.S. steel industry in 1983, I was laid off. The timing was horrible. My wife and I had just bought a new house, and we had a young child. We had a mortgage on the house, and I didn't have much savings. There was no way I was going to find a job which paid as much as I was making at the steel mill, so I knew I'd have to get creative if we were going to survive financially.

"I had never really done any art work, but I could 'doodle.' I went out one night and bought an airbrush. I spent $100 that we didn't have. My wife thought I was crazy, but I began practicing drawing with the airbrush on old bed sheets. It took me three months and a lot of sheets before I could do artwork that anyone would want to buy. But I knew that the steel mill wasn't going to call me back for a long, long time, and I knew that I had to make some changes in my short-term plans."

> When people are laid off, it's too easy to blame the company and then sit back and wait for something good to happen. Most people simply scale back their spending so that their unemployment benefits will cover their needs. A layoff can be a great incentive to set some new goals. Many overachievers have used a job layoff as an opportunity to achieve success — not as an excuse for failure.

Randy Carniak

Randy grew up as the oldest child in a working-class family. He was pretty ordinary in high school — his major interests were sports and girls. When he started college, he didn't have especially good study habits, so his grades the first two years were just average. He looks back now and realizes that he was wasting a lot of time.

A couple of things turned Randy around. He was working summers for a utility company, and he came into contact with a number of effective managers. "I realized that I could talk on the same level as they did, and I suddenly realized that I had just as much <u>potential</u> ability as the people who were my supervisors.

> As I wrote earlier, there is very little difference between highly successful people and "average" people. Start watching people who are high achievers. Look for characteristics you have in common with them.

"Also — the summer before my junior year, I saw that a lot of my friends had already dropped out of college and had gone to work at the steel mill. That's when I realized that the next two years at college would have a lot to do with the kind of job I got. For me, that was my turning point — that was all it took. I made up my mind right then to start working up to my capacity. I went back to school in the fall a changed person. I actually spent most of my time *studying*.

> America's colleges are full of people with great potential — most of whom will never discover that they can actually do much better than they are. If you're still in college, now is the best time to improve your work habits. But before you get back to your homework, read the rest of this book.

Brad Thomas

"When I was growing up, my parents had a restaurant, and that's where I really got my education. Even when I was in grade school, I would get a lot of satisfaction trying to see how many pieces of pie I could sell in a day. On Sundays, when a lot of people would eat at the restaurant after church, I'd go around to each table and say 'I stayed up all night baking a pecan pie. It has this light crust, a rich filling, and these big pecans on top. And it's still warm. Would you like a piece?' Of course, these people would know that a 12-year kid hadn't made the pie, but I described it in a way to make it seem enticing. I sold a lot of pie that way. One thing the restaurant taught me was that I could talk to anyone. I was never afraid to talk to adults.

"Several years later, my parents opened a second restaurant. My mother planned to run it, but she didn't know much about the business part, so I did everything— handling the money, ordering all the supplies, and so on. I didn't realize it then, but I was actually the restaurant manager — and I was still in high school.

"Speaking of high school ... I hated it. My graduating class had about 150 people in it, and I'm sure I finished in the lower 10%. I'd make C's and D's and an occasional B. My main interest in high school was football. Like a lot of kids my age, I had a dream of playing in college, although I wasn't big enough to do very well. I became pretty good, not because of any natural ability, but because I was a hard worker.

At college, I did play a little football, but I soon saw that I simply didn't have the desire and the intensity that the "real" athletes had. My one year of college classes — I hated every minute of it. Early in my freshman year, a friend and I started washing 18-wheel trucks on the weekend with a little pickup truck and a small washer in the back of it. When I started cutting class to clean trucks during the week, I realized that I was wasting my time in school, so I came home to my small town of 3,000 people. It was pretty obvious that college and I weren't made for each other.

"I knew that I could make money washing 18-wheelers, so I bought a used bread truck and fixed it up with a home-made high-pressure water system. I borrowed $2,500 to pay for that first truck. My father wasn't able to help me financially, since he was just trying to make ends meet with his restaurant business, so my grandfather co-signed the note at the bank for me. That easily, I was on my own, in business for myself. I decided that since I wasn't going to impress anybody with my ability in the classroom, I could impress them with my desire to be a hard worker. I decided when I was 19 that I wanted to be known as the hardest working young man in town."

Far too many people who don't do well in college will say "I failed at that" and then simply accept whatever life gives them. If college isn't your thing, set a *different* goal. More than half of all overachievers did **not** graduate from college. Many never attended college.

David Carter

I wasted a lot of time in high school, and rarely took a book home. I was a lot more interested in sports and the Boy Scouts than I was in doing homework. The Boy Scouts was actually a substitute for school for me. I found most of my classes pretty boring, but the merit badge program was a challenge for me, and I tried to get as many as I could. I had to read a lot to qualify for those awards — and I probably learned a lot more than if I had spent the same amount of time on my classes. In 9th grade, I took an interest in writing fiction, and I wrote a lot of short stories as well as non-fiction. I would write something creative just about every night (when I was supposed to be doing my homework).

Unfortunately, my Scout work and my writing didn't appear on my high school report cards. In a senior class of 97 people, I finished somewhere in the lower half. Still, I knew I was a pretty good writer, and I wanted to get a degree in journalism and be a sports writer.

A few weeks after graduation, I got a job offer, and it was very tempting. My mother had raised me by herself since I was five, and we really needed the money. I had a job offer as a clerk in a factory — the pay would have been $300 a month! Pretty good for 1960, and especially for a kid of 17.

> I was ready to "settle" for something less than what I really wanted, because I could have a job quickly, with little effort. Did you choose your career path, or did you settle for less than you wanted?

Fortunately, the job fell through. I wasn't yet 18, and the company's insurance wouldn't cover me. Since they wouldn't wait the six months until my birthday to hire me, someone else got the job.

> I often wonder what would have happened to me if I *had* been hired. Most likely, I would have never discovered the potential I had to be an entrepreneur. I think of the millions of people — with high potential — who are now locked into jobs that they had "settled" for. Did you really *want* the job you have now? Are you in a dead-end job with no real potential for advancement? Do you look at the people around you and say "I'm better than this place?" You don't have to stay there all your life, you know. The first step toward improving yourself is the decision to *change*.

I was able to get a little financial help from a newspaper editor who had seen some of my writing (but not my grades,) so I entered a two-year community college in the fall. My lack of study skills followed me from high school to college. After fall semester, I was on academic probation.

The first semester of my sophomore year was an early turning point. One afternoon, as I was wasting time in the lounge, several students were talking about their grades from a recent test. All of us had received a C on the test — myself included. As I looked at the other students, I suddenly realized "I'm smarter than any of them — but the teacher doesn't know it." I knew it was time to start working harder. The big project for class — a research paper — was my change. I had developed an interest in advertising, and chose TV commercials as my topic. I spent a lot of time on that paper, because I liked the subject.

The funny thing is, when I was doing so poorly in college, I really *believed* that I was working hard, but I was really wasting a lot of time. It was only when I began working *really* hard that I began to realize how little effort I had been using before.

Most people today are performing at about 50% or less of their capacity.

Just once, take on a project you *really like*, and commit yourself to it *completely*. Then you can see just how much you're capable of achieving.

The decision to change — to make a real change — is the starting point toward becoming an overachiever.

"Average" people can accomplish extraordinary things,

but only if they change their undesirable traits and work habits.

All the people you've met in this chapter looked at themselves, and didn't like what they saw. Then — they made the decision to do something about it — to change themselves for the better.

What traits do you have that are holding you back? Take a hard look at yourself, be honest, and then *decide to change* those things which are keeping you away from success.

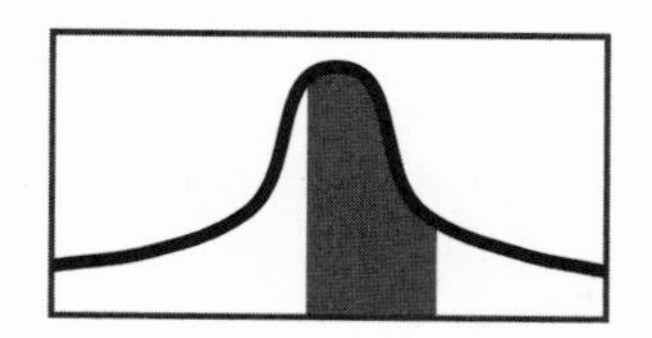

3 Dream — then set some goals.

Begin with a dream.

Before you can set goals, you need to have a dream — a big goal that actually defines what you want out of life.

Your dream might be to own your business, or to become vice president of advertising for a major company, or to work in a job that lets you travel all over the world.

> **Begin with a dream, because it gives *real* meaning to all of your efforts to become an overachiever.**

What is *your* dream?

What do you *really* want out of life? You might want to think about that for a while. While you're in the dreaming stage, be sure to keep the dream *realistic*. That big goal should be one that you can achieve *by doing things to make it happen*.

Some examples of realistic goals are:

- Open a fishing lodge at a lake resort area
- Run a successful video production business

• Start a heating/air conditioning business (while still employed) that will be large enough in 5 years so that I can quit my job.

• Buy an existing retail store, then make it grow much larger

• Start a day-care center so that I can be with my children while I work

• Becoming a top Hollywood writer (watch Jim Harris do it in this book)

• Start a service company and within 20 years, sell out to a huge company.

Avoid dreams that are <u>not</u> realistic.

Some "dreams" are dependent upon blind luck — things which you can't control. If your dream is not dependent upon your *doing things* to make it happen, try another dream.

Some dreams to avoid:

• Winning the lottery
• Being "discovered" as the next Tom Cruise
• Becoming the next Christie Brinkley
• Becoming the next Joe DiMaggio

Obviously, people win the lottery. Somebody is going to be the next Tom Cruise. (Maybe Brad Pitt is already there, but my daughters tell me that Leonardo Di Caprio is the next Brad Pitt.) The next Christie Brinkley is out there somewhere. And there will be great baseball players in the future.

But all the dreams above are pretty dependent upon things beyond your control (blind luck for the lottery, and the right combination of genes plus getting the right breaks for the others).

Your big dream should be one that you can achieve *by doing things to make it happen.* When *you* control your destiny, living the life of your dreams is much easier.

Overachievers all begin as "average people" with a dream.

Goal setting is a necessary part of achieving anything — much less *over*achieving. The problem most people have is that they **1.** set *too few* goals, and **2.** they don't set goals *often* enough.

The *under*achiever, for example, may set a goal of simply keeping an existing job for another year without getting fired. That's simply a "maintenance" goal; as in "I want to maintain only what I have." While that's certainly a worthy goal, it's not very *ambitious.*

A better goal (quite typical) would be to get a promotion to a higher pay grade within the year.

But a potential overachiever might have a goal which involves finishing a career-related educational goal, which provides the skills to make better business decisions, which might lead to a promotion to branch manager, which will lead to more goals — and more opportunities.

Notice that the typical goal (getting a promotion to a higher pay grade) is a *single-point* goal, with no continuing effect or action. However, the goal of the potential overachiever above is a *multi-level* goal: (1. finishing career-related education, which leads to 2. better decision-making skills, which leads to 3. a significant promotion, which leads to 4. another level of opportunities).

What kind of goals do *you* have?

This would be a good time to begin thinking about some things which you want to accomplish. Write them down. The *written plan* is important, because it shows more of a commitment than a mental goal does. Next, list the things you have to do to *reach* that goal. Then, list the possible results of reaching that goal. (See the example below.)

Your goals don't have to be career-related. Just getting into a goal setting habit is important. I have a goal of breaking 80 for 18 holes of golf. Below is my written plan that is mentioned above.

Goal: Break 80 on the golf course

How do I reach this goal:

1. Get instruction from a golf pro.
2. Practice my short game
3. Practice my long game
4. Practice my putting.

Results of reaching my goal:

1. Playing golf will be even more enjoyable.
2. I'll have a shot at a trophy in the club championship.
3. I'll have the confidence to play Pebble Beach. (I'm not going to pay $200 to shoot a 95!)

This personal golf gols of mine is a fairly simple example of how to get into the habit of setting goals. Once you do that, goal setting becomes a way of life for you. It doesn't matter if your goal is job related or a personal one (such as raising some delicious tomatoes next summer), goal setting is the key to getting anything done.

If most of your goals are single-level, that's OK — for now. The most important thing is to set goals often. The other factor is to set goals which are attainable, but high enough to challenge you. You might set a goal of being on time for work every day. That's a nice thought, but it's not much of a challenge. (In fact, in most places, it's kind of expected.) A more worthy goal may be to complete all your written reports a day ahead of time — so that you'll have time to re-write them and make them better before turning them in, which will make you a more productive employee. (Notice that this is a multi-level goal, where achieving one goal leads to the accomplishment of another one.)

Once you begin setting (and reaching) goals frequently, start to set goals that are a bit tougher — and with a longer-range time frame. And as you read about the next steps for our cast of overachievers, notice how they began setting goals.

Jim Harris

One night while watching the Johnny Carson show, Jim Harris heard one of his jokes in Carson's monologue. The only problem was that Jim had just written the joke a few minutes earlier. Rather than being discouraged, Jim was suddenly elated. A joke he had written was good enough to be on network TV!

Jim remembers those days well. "Right then, I decided that I wanted to hear Johnny read a joke that I had sent to him. I began working harder and harder, spending more time reading the daily newspapers to find good subject matter. I spent several hours a day writing material for the show. For a while, I didn't tell anybody about my big dream.
It was so silly — I was living in a small town , and I didn't even know anybody in show business. It seemed like such an impossible dream. But I kept writing every day."

Jim didn't know it at the time, but he had just set a multi-level goal. (1. Write a joke that is so good that 2. Johnny Carson will read it on the air.) And he had set an "all or nothing goal." That is, either Johnny Carson *would* read his joke on the air or he *wouldn't*. There's no middle ground, no "near miss" which can be construed as success. (The person who sets a goal of making $10,000 in sales in a month can have a "near miss" by selling $9,950 and still be very successful.) But Bob's goal was going to be either bull's eye — or a total miss.

He had formulated a series of *intermediate goals* on his way to reaching his ultimate goal: having his work on the Johnny Carson show. The intermediate goals were something like this: **1.** practice writing every day to get better at it, so that he could **2.** produce a quantity of funny material virtually every day, which was good enough **3.** to let Jim choose the jokes with the most promise which **4.** Jim would type and send to Johnny Carson, who would **5.** Read the jokes, and like one well enough to **6.** Read it on the air.

Obviously, Jim never took the time to write out his goal outline the way someone would diagram a sentence. Come to think of it, Jim hadn't exactly been spending a lot of his time diagramming sentences recently.

The important thing to remember is that Jim set a multi-level goal, and then did everything which was necessary to make the first few steps translate from wish to reality.

Think about your hopes and dreams for a minute. What kind of multi-level goals could you set which would advance you toward some ultimate accomplishment? Take a minute to *write down* your possible steps toward reaching some long-range goal. (Don't worry. You don't have to turn this in for a grade, and there's no points taken off for misspelled words.)

David Warren

David had to literally beg for a chance to be admitted to a community college, but once he was in, he formulated a multi-step goal. "Even though I was in the 2-year physical therapy associate degree program, I immediately set a goal to receive a 4-year baccalaureate degree. I knew I'd have to do well in order to get into a larger school. I got a 3.7 that first semester, and finished the two-year degree, graduating cum laude. As soon as I got into physical therapy school (at the University of Kentucky) I began planning my clinical work. When I saw the "real" physical therapists working, I decided I wanted to do *more* than they were doing — and to do it better. I was still a student, but I wanted much more of myself than I saw others attaining. I made notes on things I felt I could improve upon. I was barely in my third year of college, and I was making career plans for several years ahead."

David wasn't content to be average. He set goals for himself, and worked to reach those goals.

Teresa Wright

"As the date for the real estate exam got closer, I couldn't wait to get back to the city, so I moved before I took the test. I was already setting a lot of real estate career goals for myself, but while I was waiting to take the exam, I had to support myself. Since I didn't have my real estate license yet, I got a job with an accounting firm. It was quickly obvious *to everyone* that I was not cut out to be an accountant; they fired me.* Then, I failed the real estate examination by one point. *One point.* What a start. My first goal was to get my real estate license, and I now had to wait to take the exam all over again. But that didn't stop my goal setting. By the time I passed the exam, I had already made contact with a local Realtor, who let me take their sales classes while I was studying for my second test.

*Not uncommon. A lot of overachievers were fired from jobs for a variety of reasons. Getting fired is just another item on the "permanent record" which means *nothing* when the big picture is considered.

"One of the things I learned in real estate school was that you need a 4-door car to show properties to prospects. The week I got my license, I bought a new 1984 Chrysler New Yorker. A lady who had been selling for ten years said 'that's a beautiful car, but how are you going to pay for it?'"

"That was the least of my concerns. I would constantly re-read my sales manuals, and I worked a 40-hour week — something a lot of people in real estate don't do. After I had been with the firm for several months, I got an offer from a larger firm. Although I was put into a location where the typical home price was $40,000, I sold more than $3 million my first year. [Author's note: That's several times the national average for *all* real estate salespeople — not just beginners. People brag in their ads when they sell *one* million in a year.] I became extremely goal oriented, and reaching those goals became very important to me."

Randy Carniak

When Randy returned to college to start his junior year, he didn't realize it then, but he had set a multi-stage goal. "I wanted to see if I could get a 4.0 for the semester. Then, I wanted to keep doing as well as I could until I graduated. I figured if I had mostly all A's my last two years, I could get a job with a larger corporation. That was one of my big goals — I wanted to work for a large company where I had a lot of room to advance. I felt that I wouldn't be able to reach my potential if I took a typical entry-level job for a small business."

Mal Charles

"My first goal was simply to survive the layoff from the steel mill. I was making good money while I was working, but the layoff put a dent in my income. Even though I was getting SUB-pay (supplemental unemployment benefits) I had a significant drop in income with the layoff. Once I learned how to use the airbrush, I started taking it to weekend flea markets, and I would custom design T-shirts. I'd draw someone's car, or put their name on the shirt in a fancy script, or whatever they wanted.
"Pretty soon, my goal changed. Where I simply wanted to survive the

layoff at first, I made longer range goals. I wanted to improve my drawing skills, which would help me sell more. I also wanted to make additional contacts to get into more places, such as carnivals, which would give me larger crowds of possible buyers. And I wanted to improve my skills as a businessman, so I could manage the success that I was certain was coming my way."

Mal didn't realize he was setting multi-level goals, but he was. In addition, he had several different goals at the same time (becoming a better businessman; making additional contacts, etc.)

"I wanted to build a reputation in the show painting business. It was something I liked to do, and as I got better the money came along fairly soon. Before long, I was pretty well established among the people who runs shows and carnivals. I was spending a lot of time on the road, but six months after I was laid off, I was making more money than I had been at the steel mill.

"Now, I realize that you *must* have written goals, and a written business plan. But even then, I was writing down my goals."

During the two years he was laid off from his job at the steel mill, Mal made a lot of contacts, worked in a lot of places, and was actually making a lot more money than he ever had earned at his old job. But everything changed when he was called back to work.

"Going back to my old job was the biggest mistake I ever made. I did it for the security and the benefits. But several years later, the plant eventually closed some departments, and a lot of people lost their jobs permanently. I was one of those people. In looking back now, I should never have gone back to work. All it did was slow down my progress. And I discovered something important about job security — the only job security is *no* job security. Anyone who is on a payroll can be laid off. But the entrepreneur — he can always make something happen to generate income."

Has your company downsized yet? Do you really have job security? What would you do if you lost your job tomorrow?

Brad Thomas

"My little business was certainly no overnight success. To be honest, it was a struggle for a while. One difficulty was that I'd make money in the summer, but I'd lose it in the winter. The truck washing business was very seasonal; there just weren't enough warm days to wash trucks outdoors in January and February. And since my equipment was so basic, I couldn't get any cleaning jobs other than washing trucks. I kept wondering what I could do to make more money. The first big turn-around for me came during the Johnstown (Pennsylvania) flood about 20 years ago. The town had been flooded so badly that they needed every piece of cleaning equipment that they could get. I took a couple of pickup trucks up there and for the first time, I saw what high-end high-pressure vacuum trucks were about. I saw trucks that had 10 times the pressure and power of my little truck and I immediately said "that's the kind of cleaning equipment I want to have." Once I saw what the big boys had, I decided to be one of them. That was my big goal. That was my *dream.*

> I wonder how many other small operators like Brad went to Johnstown, saw the big trucks, but simply thought "The guy who owns those sure is lucky." Brad saw the big trucks— and set a goal to have one.

"Goals are so important. Can you imagine building a skyscraper without having a blueprint? If you're going on a long trip, you need street signs along the way — to show you how you're progressing in your goals. I think it's important to write down the goals, and look at them. That doesn't mean you can't change your goals, but you need to have a written plan. Goals are a benchmark of success.

"When I was just beginning to grow my little business, I would love to set goals — and then reach them. Even when I was struggling with one pickup truck, I always wanted a nice big office and an airplane. I'd watch TV and see businessmen get off private airplanes. To me, the company plane was a sign of success. Even when I was doing a lot of the cleaning work myself, I knew that someday I'd have a company plane. The important thing is to avoid setting goals that are <u>too</u> high — so high that you can't reach them. But you need to set goals high enough that you have to push yourself to get there."

David Carter

The paper I wrote on TV commercials received an A, but my other grades in the class pulled it down, so that I got a B+ for the semester. Encouraged by my new study habits, I decided to go for an A in the new term. (That was a pretty high goal, since the only A that I made in high school had been in Physical Education.) Somehow, I managed to get the A in a speech class. That accomplishment gave my self confidence a real boost. The day that I got an A in speech, I knew that I was going to be a college graduate. (Up until then, I had my doubts.) That became my next big goal. (Every class was a sub-goal; a career was the result of reaching my big goal.)

> It's amazing how reaching even one goal can inspire you to set even higher goals. Try it. Before long, setting (and reaching) goals becomes part of your personality.

At some point along the way, I finally learned how to study. Even so, I would occasionally lapse into my old habits. In my "fun classes" — things in my major, like TV Advertising and Magazine Advertising, I made A's. But in things such as Geology and Astronomy, I pulled down a couple of D's. Anyway, my overall grades were good enough to get me admitted to the master's degree program at Ohio University, where I really caught fire an made all A's except for one B[*].

After graduate school, I was 24 years old and landed a nice cozy job teaching advertising and communications at a community college. I had

[*]Almost everyone in that class "borrowed" term papers which had earned A's in previous years. I chose not to do that, and "earned" my B. I'm very proud of that B.

gone from "average student" to college teacher. I had reached my ultimate goal. I could teach a few hours a week, and do a few advertisements on the side and have a nice simple life. "I have worked very hard to get here," I told myself, "and now I can rest." I figured that I had reached my maximum potential. (I was wrong.)

A word about goal setting.

Below is the text of an advertisement that I saw when I was in college. I liked it so much that I had it framed and kept it in my room throughout my college years. (It's been in my office ever since.)

Reach for the Stars.

You might not quite get one,

but you won't come up with a handful of mud, either.

Advertisement for the Leo Burnett Co., an advertising agency

The importance of written goals

Some research has shown that having a *written* career plan has a dramatic impact upon salary levels. Several years ago, I read a study that compared the career plan strategy of entrepreneurs and their annual incomes.

In this study, entrepreneurs were asked "How did you plan your business career?"

The possible responses were:

1. I had no plan. Things happened, and I responded to the changes and opportunities as I saw fit.

2. I had a career plan in mind all the time.

3. I had a written career plan, which I revised whenever conditions changed.

The people in this study then were asked to give their annual income. The impact of career planning upon annual income is highly dramatic, as the chart below shows.

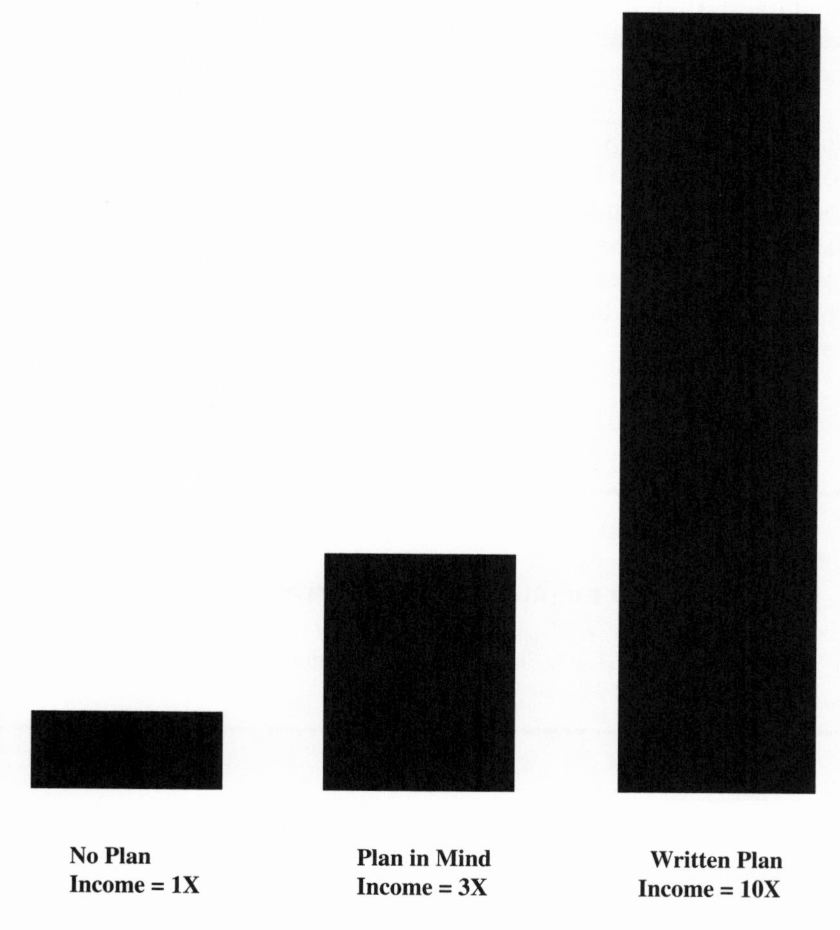

No Plan
Income = 1X

Plan in Mind
Income = 3X

Written Plan
Income = 10X

*I read this somewhere several years ago, but didn't write down the source. I've quoted these numbers several times since that, but I don't have any idea where this information came from. I just *know* that I saw it. You'll have to trust me on this one. (I know, this would count off if this book were a term paper. But it's not a term paper. OK?)

The research found that entrepreneurs with no plan had the lowest income; those with a "plan in mind" had *three times* the income of the "no plan" group, while those with a *written plan* had *10 times* the income as the "no plan" group. I know of no better argument for having a *written* plan.

Don't lose sight of your goals.

It's awfully easy to get sidetracked. I went to college with a bright young woman who majored in advertising and who had very high ambitions. All of her classmates knew that she was going to really do well in her field. But when I saw her ten years after graduation, she told me she was a secretary.

She summed up her work history with a sound of defeat in her voice. "I couldn't find the job I wanted, so I took the secretarial position only until something better came along. But after a while, I became comfortable in the job, got a couple of raises, and eventually stopped looking for something else." Her voice trailed off as she finished the sentence. It's obvious that all the dreams she once had have been misplaced — perhaps never to be found.

> **If you don't know where you're going,**
>
> **you might wind up somewhere else.**
>
> Casey Stengel, 20th century philosopher and baseball manager

> Have you "settled" for a job (and a life) that is less than what you really want? It's not too late to start changing. How would you like to improve your life? What would you have to change about yourself in order to make that improvement happen? Set some goals now that will start you toward those life changes.

Reality check.

You're now almost halfway through this book. Now is a good time to ask yourself some questions.

1. **Are you content to be just "average?"**
2. **Do you often have ideas for new products or services?**
3. **Do you look at your place of work and see improvements you would make if you were "in charge?"**
4. **Do you feel frustrated working with people who have less drive than you do?**
5. **Are you content with the money you now make?**
6. **Do you sometimes see "successful" people and think to yourself "I'm just as smart as that person?"**
7. **Are you now on "the road of success?"**
8. **Will you be one of those people who grows old and says "you know — I could have been ..."**
9. **Are you willing to leave your "comfort zone?"**
10. **Have you decided to *do something* with your life?**

You will now discover that unlike many "self tests" in magazines and books, there are no "answers" given here. Those of you who are truly ready to move toward becoming an overachiever will *know* what the answers are. Those who are not willing to take that step simply won't understand, even if all the answere are given.

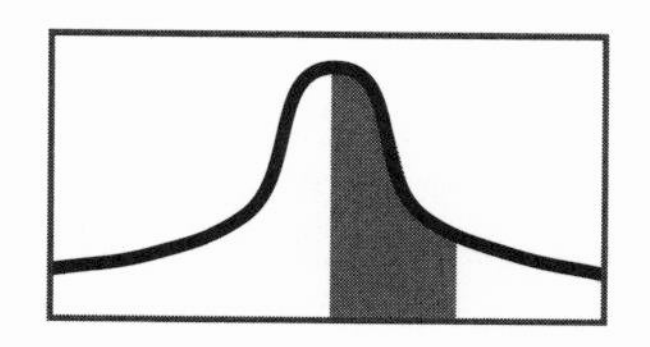

4. Start listening. People will tell you how to succeed.

"Did you invent that product?"

"No."

Why are you so successful?"

"I sell it to people. Lots of people want it."

"How did you know they wanted to buy it?"

"They told me."

It's amazing how many ideas you'll get if you simply listen. The most successful people are often those who have learned to listen. This chapter will show how our cast of overachievers has learned about the road to success — just by listening.

Jim Harris

While Jim had set a very high goal — becoming a writer for the Johnny Carson Show — he also needed to see if he really had what it took to be a comedy writer. I should mention here that this was about at this same time that I first met Jim. My earliest memories of him were that he was working as a part-time clerk in a super market. Frequently, Jim would pop in to my office (unannounced), and say something like: "Have you heard the newest Bob Newhart comedy album?" Then, he'd do a 30-minute monologue of very funny stand-up comedy. A few weeks later, he'd be back and say "Have you heard the newest Bill Cosby comedy album?" I'd say "no," and Jim would then launch another 30 minutes of really funny material. At that time, I had no idea that there was *no* new comedy album — but *all the material was written by Jim.* This was his way of testing his ability as a comedy writer. And, he was *listening* — to the response of people who thought his comedy was the work of somebody already famous in the business.

Jim looks back on those days: "I would write about 30 minutes of comedy, which back then would take me about a week. I really needed for someone else to tell me if it was funny or not. But how do you *do* that? If I told someone 'here's some stuff I've written — tell me if it's funny'— that's not really a good test. People will tell you what they think you *want* to hear. But when I would ask somebody 'have you heard the latest Bill Cosby album,' and then do 30 minutes of stuff I had written, they would think they were laughing at Cosby's material — not mine. When I could make people laugh that way, I knew I could write comedy at a fairly high level. I simply listened to their laughter, and I knew I could do it."

Author's note: I liked the newest "Bob Newhart album" so much that I tried to buy it. When I discovered that there was no "new album" by Bob Newhart — that's when I realized that Jim was the comedy writer. He was writing comedy from his personal experience — and it was really good. When I told Jim that I had looked for the Newhart album — he confessed. "You caught me," he said, a little sheepishly. From that point on, I knew about his dream to write for the Carson show.

David Warren

David was seeing a very large number of railroad workers who were coming into the physical therapy clinic to have back injuries treated. "Many of the injuries I saw came from people doing seemingly simple tasks. When I would mention that there were a lot of back injuries among railroad workers, several of the patients said 'you'd think that they would try to do something to *prevent* this type injury from happening.' I suddenly realized that this was a need that wasn't being filled. I went to my boss with the idea of our doing back injury *prevention* training. I did some research and found there was only one program in the world that stressed prevention of back injuries. It was in Sweden, but it was teaching an old technology. We decided we could do it better. I *knew* there was a huge market for teaching back injury prevention to industrial workers. I knew it because I *listened* to what people — workers with back injuries — were saying."

Teresa Wright

Teresa Wright discovered one step to success was by hosting open houses. She knew this was an effective sales tool in other markets, but noticed that there were only a few open houses hosted by real estate sales people in her area. "I started doing open houses when no one else in town was. One open house on a Sunday wasn't enough for me — I'd do *two* on the same afternoon. Other real estate salespeople wanted to have Sunday afternoon off. But that's when prospective buyers want to go house hunting. When the customer wants something, you succeed if you fill that want. So, I became the open house queen. It worked very well for me. I simply looked at what was working in other places, and did it in the community where I lived."

The lesson to be learned from Teresa Wright is very important. She didn't invent anything; she simply looked at what *other* successful people were doing that was not being done in her area. Then *she* did it. Remember her statement from the previous paragraph: when the customer wants something, you succeed if you fill that want.

You don't have to *own or create* an idea in order to become successful. Some of the simplest — and most certain — paths to success are those that have already been taken by other successful people.

Randy Carniak

Randy persistently pursued a job with a local clothing factory — with its home office in New York City. He kept visiting the personnel department so often that he developed a first-name relationship with the person in charge of hiring.

"I was able to show the personnel manager that I really wanted to work for the company, so he finally hired me. I was a trainee and started in the customer service department. My first assignment was to solve a lot of customer problems. Very quickly, I discovered the value of listening. As I talked to the customers, I saw a pattern of complaints. Then, I asked the customers for suggestions on how we might avoid similar problems in the future. I was really amazed when customers began telling me changes that we could make. The typical response was 'Company X has a really good shipping control system. You should do it like they do.' So I'd call the shipping manager at Company X and tell them I was trying to improve our system. I'd tell him that I was new on the job, and mention that a customer had praised his system, and ask for help.

"I made some major improvements in the customer service department that way. I didn't know enough to make the changes myself. I simply listened to the customers. Then I called companies who had already solved problems like we were having. It didn't take a genius to make the changes. I just listened to people.

"The increased efficiency of my department was noticed by the right people. Everyone knew I was responsible, and I got a quick promotion as a result. I learned a lot from that experience. I listened to successful people, and did what they were doing."

Mal Charles

Mal was turning away so much business with his airbrush art that he *had* to expand. "Customers would ask for specific items — they would tell me what designs they wanted. If you listen, you'll see a pattern to customer requests. You can simply base your work on customer ideas. No one person has enough knowledge to make all these decisions without listening to customers. But the first time someone says "do you have ......" and the answer is no. You make a mental note. The second time you get the same request, you really start to think. By the third time you get a request, your answer should be 'I'll have it in a couple of weeks. Can I take your order now?"

Listen. People really will tell you how to succeed.

Brad Thomas

"I was always aware of the limitations I had. My lack of a college education was always in the back of mind. So I realized that I had to look *everywhere* for good business ideas. I don't care if it's analyzing the Girl Scout cookie sale, or listening to my wife talking, or reading a magazine article. You have to be able to recognize good ideas when you hear them. Then, you have to realize that you don't have to be responsible for every idea. A lot of budding entrepreneurs think every idea should be their own. But the really smart people know that good ideas come from *anywhere*.

"Just because I didn't go to college doesn't mean that I didn't continue my education. I read a lot of articles, and watched what the competition was doing. I watched other successful business, and I listened to my financial advisors. Doing all those things literally taught me a lot of the steps to becoming successful. In meetings, I didn't talk a lot — I mostly listened. You learn a lot more listening than you do talking."

Brad Thomas became a master of listening to his customers. Every major expansion he made into a new area of industrial cleaning was due to listening to a customer. He would have a crew in a plant doing a certain type of cleaning when someone from the plant's management would ask if he did *another* type job. Brad would never say no. The customer would express a need and Brad would find an expert in that area and hire him. That's how he got into the asbestos removal business — and the chemical cleaning business — and the vacuum cleaning business, and several others.

Customers would simply tell Brad that they had a need, and he would expand his business to fill that need. But he was careful *not* to expand outside his area of expertise.

"As long as it was in the industrial cleaning business, when I saw an opportunity, I expanded into that area. But I always resisted the temptation to expand into an area where we would be total rookies. That would be an invitation to failure."

Every day, people will tell you how to be successful.

All you have to do is listen. And then — act.

David Carter

When I was 27 years old, I was teaching at the local community college and hadn't yet discovered that an entrepreneur was inside me — just waiting to get out.

I was teaching a class in advertising design. Chapter 13 in the book was about logos. After class one day, a student came up to me with a simple question: "Where can I find a book that shows hundreds of logos?"

I had a mental picture of what such a book might look like. In fact, I wanted to find a book like that, too. "I'll find a logo book and bring it to class next week," I told her. But after checking with two libraries (plus the directory *Books in Print)*, I came up empty handed. The second librarian told me "there's nothing like that available." When I heard those words, a light came on in my head. "*I'll* do that book," I thought.

Within a week, I began collecting well-designed logos and began sending a form letter to companies with good logos, asking for their permission to include their logo in my book. Before long, I had collected hundreds of logos for my book. Eventually, I had nearly 1,000.

My book was finally ready for the world, so I wrote to 17 major publishers, telling them about what I had. I got back 17 rejection letters. The few that bothered with a personal note said something like "there's no market for your book." Discouraged, I put the book on a closet shelf for months. I knew it was a good idea. But when 17 publishers tell you that your idea is no good, it's a discouraging experience. But in the back of my mind, the fact that "there's no book like this" meant that there *was* a market for my book.

You're not always going to have immediate success. But if you treat every setback as a learning experience, future success becomes much more likely.

Listen to yourself

Today, one of my businesses markets a software product (Logo SuperPower®, which helps create high-quality logos.) I had been involved in the logo design business for a number of years when the computer revolution changed all the rules. I finally joined the revolution and bought a Macintosh. When it was installed, I asked the sales rep "where's the logo design software?" He said, "I don't think there's any product made just for creating logos." I thought about that for a few weeks, and realized that there must be *hundreds* of people like me who wanted a logo design software product. (I was wrong: there were thousands.) Six weeks after I bought my first Macintosh, I got the idea of how a logo design software system would work. Less than eleven weeks later, my new product was on the market, and I was in the software business. In this case, **I simply listened to myself. I needed a product that didn't exist, so I created it.**

Start listening to yourself.
Whenever you have a need for something and can't find it,
that's a sign of a business opportunity for someone.
Why shouldn't that someone be YOU?

• A friend of mine couldn't find a "classy" affordable restaurant for lunch near her business. So, she started one in an under-utilized part of her retail store. The result: a profitable restaurant, and increased sales for her primary business, due to the increased lunch traffic.

• An acquaintance of mine bought an old car and wanted to restore it. When he couldn't find someone to do it, he did it himself. Today, he has a lucrative business — restoring old cars for people.

• Another friend (a Civil War buff) wanted an authentic-looking cannon to sit in front of his antebellum home. When he discovered that there were only a couple of firms making these items, he decided to make one himself. It turned out so well that he started a business making cannons. (People actually pay up to $26,000 for one of his cannons!)

• A married couple I've known for years bought and re-decorated a beautiful old home. When they couldn't find the kind of interior items they wanted, they started a store which specializes in items from other countries. Besides getting to make business trips overseas, they make a nice profit!

You'll find ideas everywhere.
A lot of them will be floating around in your own head.

Start keeping a notebook with you. Whenever you want something that you can't find, write it down. Before long, you're going to find a market need that is not being filled. Sooner or later, you'll discover one that *you* can fill. And that is how average people begin to become overachievers.

Sometimes, all it takes to become a major success
is to listen to yourself.
When Stephen Spielberg was asked about
the "secret" of his success, he replied
"I make the movies that I would like to have seen as a kid."

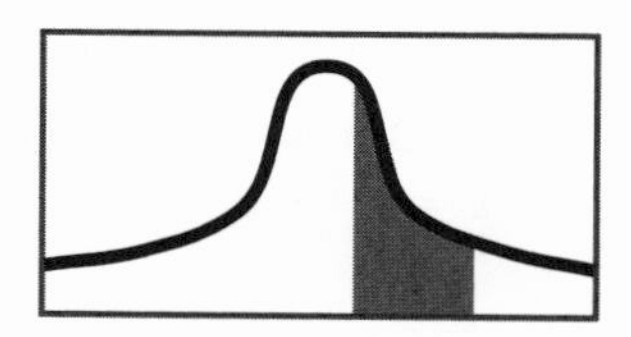

5. Take action!

> **The person who has ability and doesn't *use* it**
>
> **is no better off than the person who has *no* ability.**

Take action! For some reason, this is the tough part for so many people. Most people want to improve themselves (or so they say), and they spend a lot of time sitting and *thinking* about it a lot. And they *dream* about what they'll do once they've achieved all this success. (They even plan the interior of the yacht, and imagine how they'll decorate the beach front condo! The only problem is — they're dreaming without *action*.)

The one thing most people *don't* do is *act*. They never get off their duff and take the *action* that is needed to make something good happen to them.

> **Success is not a noun — it's a verb**

I once had a great teacher at the University of Kentucky who would always say the same thing before exams. "I wish you *luck* on the test," she'd say. Then she'd pause and say "Of course, you know that luck is what happens when preparation meets opportunity." I kept that thought with me for many years. But recently, I've modified it.

Formula for Luck
L = P + L x A

Luck = Preparation + Opportunity X (multiplied by) Action

All the highly successful people I know are *very* lucky (by this definition). Their good luck is the result of Preparation ... with the addition of Opportunity, multiplied by Action. Notice that the biggest factor (the *multiplier*) is Action. If you have an *opportunity,* and you are *prepared* for it, there is the *potential* for something very good to happen to you. But unless you take *action*, forget it.

You can't win the lottery if you don't buy a ticket.

This is not my endorsement of legalized gambling, but a graphic way of showing the importance of taking the action step to reach your goals. Even if you pick the right lottery numbers, if you don't act and buy the ticket, you're a loser.

The overachievers in this book all *prepared* themselves, then they met with *opportunity* for success. But without their taking the *action* step, nothing would have happened.

Jim Harris

Once Jim Harris formulated his plan, he followed the conventional advice to aspiring writers: "if you want to be a writer — write." Jim wrote comedy material for several hours every day. This part alone sets him apart from literally thousands of "funny" people. They expect that their "talent" will be all they need to attain "success." They never give a thought to doing the work (*action* word) that is required to become successful.

After months of writing comedy every day, (and testing the jokes on friends), Jim Harris finally felt prepared to put together a package of monologue jokes to send to the Johnny Carson Show. (This was 1969, when the program was still in New York City.)

Jim recalls, "I had an old manual typewriter that I wrote on, and one night I gathered all my best stuff, and began re-typing it. At that time, I had no idea of how to present jokes on paper — at first I thought I'd do it like a term paper. (That was a stretch for me, since I obviously hadn't done too many term papers recently.) I had a total of 30 or 35 jokes on five or six pages. That night, I watched the Carson show until the credits rolled at the end. I wrote down the name of the writer in the middle of the list. I figured he wasn't the newest guy on the staff, an he probably hadn't been there the longest, either. My heart was pounding as I dropped that package in the mail the next morning. About ten days later, I got all my jokes back, with a note that said something like 'we have our own writing staff, and don't accept submissions from outside the network.' Then, within a week, four of the jokes I had written were on the show, in Johnny's monologue. Instead of being mad, I was *ecstatic*. Someone had read my stuff, and liked it well enough to use it. I started working even harder. A few weeks later, I sent in some more jokes — to the same writer who had received the material before.

"This time, I got a personal note that said 'your work is getting better. Keep practicing.' That really got me going. I was creating comedy material almost every waking minute. A week or two later, I sent about 15 pages to my writing contact at the Carson show.

"I got a nice handwritten note back saying that my work was quite professional, and inviting me to 'stop by and talk comedy writing' if I was ever in New York.

"That was all I needed. The next day, I went to the bank, borrowed $100 for a train ticket , and left the next evening. All during the train ride, I tried to tell myself not to expect too much. After all, I was 22 years old, and my 'day job' was part-time salesman in a men's store. By the time I got there, my big ambition was to get a free ticket to the show, and maybe meet Ed McMahon."

By the time Jim left the NBC studios, he had met all the writers, lunched with Ed McMahon, and even had a brief encounter with Johnny Carson himself.

"One of the people said that Johnny wanted to meet me. It never occurred to me that this was part of a job interview process. I walked into Johnny Carson's office and my only thought was wait till the people back home hear that I met Johnny Carson.' Ten minutes later, he was asking me if I could start writing for the show on Monday.

"When I look back on that experience, I realize that sometimes ignorance can be your friend. I was too naive to realize that a 22-year-old kid without writing experience had no chance of being hired by Johnny Carson. But I pursued my goal — and it happened."

This was just the start for Jim Harris. For nearly 30 years, he's had a fulfilling career as one of the most respected creative minds in Hollywood.

> Let's turn the clock back a little to when Jim first realized he was funny — *very* funny. What if he hadn't set a high goal? What if he hadn't taken the "action step" and sent his material to the Tonight Show? Have you ever wanted to do something really meaningful, but hesitated to take the action step? What kept you from taking action?

Jim grimaces when he contemplates what his life would have been like if he hadn't sent his jokes to the Carson show. "I would have been the funniest part-time clothing salesman in the world.[1] And probably the least happy."

> Are you *actively* making the most of your abilities? Remember: having ability and *not using it* produces the same result as if you had *no ability* at all. Are you taking the <u>action</u> that is needed to move toward your goals?

[1] Jim once sold me a green plaid suit. I have since forgiven him.

David Warren

When David got the idea for teaching back injury prevention techniques to industrial workers, that was the beginning of The American Back School. His *preparation* for the moment was done by becoming an expert on back injuries; the *opportunity* came when he listened to industrial workers wishing for a prevention program.) The action step was next.

"Once the idea was there, it took literally months of preparation. My boss and I had to write the material to be taught, then we had to make slides, we had to write and produce a video, and we had to literally write a book to give to each person who took our course. At that time, I was still working all day as a clinical physical therapist. I'd work 9 or 10 hours at the clinic, then work another eight hours at home, preparing materials for the back school.

"It was a very ambitious plan. We wanted to become a national company. What made it happen for us was a written schedule of all the things that had to be done and when they had to be finished. Once all the materials were finished, we were ready to move.

"In the first couple of years, I personally trained more than 10,000 workers. I was still in my twenties then, and I thought I could train the world. Before long, though, the constant teaching became a grind. That was when I began teaching the injury prevention techniques to other health care professionals, as well as corporate safety people. The 'train the trainer' program eventually went all over the United States, and was quite successful.

"In my travels, I'd occasionally meet a physical therapist who would say something like 'I had an idea about doing a program like this, but just never got around to it.' It was those times that made me realize the value of action."

Talent and ideas are as common as sand on the beach.

Success requires talent, ideas and ACTION.

Teresa Wright

Teresa Wright is a master of taking *action* (while most other real estate agents are content to *wait* for something to happen). She had the courage to act when she began studying for her real estate exam, and she had the courage to move to the city before she had passed her exam. Throughout her career, she has been a person who takes action to do more than the client expects. A *lot* more.

One anecdote about a recent sale gives a wonderful picture of just what makes Teresa Wright successful. She smiles as she tells the story. "I recently had a former client who was moving to a smaller town. The real estate broker there had only three houses listed in the $300,000 range. My former client didn't like any of them; nonetheless, the other broker said 'which one do you want to buy?'"

"My former client called me and said 'the problem is that there isn't a Teresa Wright in Winchester.' I thought about that for a second, and said "there is now." He and his wife drove me to Winchester and I said 'which neighborhood do you want to live in?' They drove me to a nice area, and I said 'stop the car.' I got out and knocked on the door at eight houses. Four of the owners agreed to sell their home if the price was right. My client looked at two of the homes, fell in love with one, and the deal was closed two weeks later. The thing is — *any* real estate agent could have done that, but they chose not to. When you give service like that, you make a client for life — and the word gets around."

In the opening part of the book, I described Teresa Wright as a "Real Estate Superstar." Others share my opinion. In the last two years, she was among Century 21's Top 100 producers in the entire U.S* and she was recently inducted into the Century 21 Hall of Fame for her high sales production. Everyone could learn a few things from Teresa Wright.

*There are over 2,100 Century 21 offices, and probably 20 times that number of sales people.

Randy Carniak

Randy's big step up the corporate ladder began six years ago — when he was 29 years old. He was in a Friday afternoon meeting with a number of sales and marketing people.

"I was the youngest person in the room. Near the end of the meeting, the company president mentioned briefly that he was thinking about the golf apparel market. He felt that this was a nice fit with our exiting business, and asked if anyone in the room knew anything about golf clothing, or about the golf market in general. Nobody said anything.

"As soon as the meeting was over, I made a few notes, then changed my weekend plans. Ironically, I was supposed to play golf both days. I went to the library on Saturday morning and began researching the golf market. I quickly got data on the number of golf courses in the country, their rapid growth rate, the number of golfers, the amount of money spent on golf clothing each year, and a lot of other data. Then I did some analysis.

"By Monday morning, I had written a 25-page report on the golf apparel market. I went in to see the company president and said, 'I spent some time over the weekend researching the potential of the golf market for us. Here's what I found.' I gave him the report.

"Four weeks later, in another meeting with the same people as before, the company president announced that we were entering the golf market. He also named me marketing manager of the new division, which shocked everyone. I was the youngest person there. But I had shown the president that I wanted the job. I took action in doing that report, while everyone else just sat around thinking about it."

Anyone in the room could have done what Randy did. But only *he* did it. You don't have to be a genius to succeed. Often, it simply requires taking action when everyone else is sitting there doing nothing.

Mal Charles

Mal had become fairly successful selling his T- shirt artwork on the carnival circuit and at weekend flea markets. But the constant travel and the odd hours did not fit with his personal goals.

"I knew that I had a big market, and I was simply taking my products to where the people were. Finally, it occurred to me that a lot of people were also in malls. So I went to see about getting a small space in the mall — for a weekend, on a trial basis. I did that, we were successful, so I signed up for the next four weekends. That worked, and sales were very high, so I decided to expand my space, and I took a six-month contract. I was doing so well (I was chosen store of the year at the mall) that they offered me a much larger space. Suddenly, I had as much square footage in the mall as the Benetton shop, or the big national chains, like Camelot Music and Foot Locker.

"One morning I was opening my store, and I thought about all the talented people who started just like I did. Most of them were still right where they started. They were still doing airbrush painting on T-shirts; they were still at flea markets. I had a large retail store with high-speed color embroidery machines as well as other custom equipment. The only difference between them and me was that I had the courage to go for something better."

> Do you have a "sideline" business that might grow much larger? What action is needed to make this possible? Are you willing to take this action?

Brad Thomas

"For a number of years, my company grew at an annul rate of more than 100%. To do that, I had to constantly take the "action step" and expand. A lot of people were impressed by our high rate of growth, but most people don't realize that opportunities come by every day. Once I saw an opportunity to expand, I would first ask myself if the new business fit with our strategic plan Then, I would ask if I can find and hire people with expertise. Finally, I would ask if I have the capital available to make the expansion.

"Other people who started off like I did were still doing the same thing that I *used* to do. A lot of them were certainly "smarter" than I was. But I would look at a possible expansion, evaluate the risk involved, and if it looked good, I'd do it."

If Brad had simply said "my little truck washing business is doing OK. Why expand?" he would have never risen above being "average." What opportunities do **you** have to take action and improve yourself?

"I like to be second miler. I like to do more than you paid me to do. If I ask you to clean off the kitchen table, and you also clean the chairs and sweep the floor, you've done more than I paid you to do. I want you to keep working for me. That's the way I've always run my business. I do *more* than people expect, and they keep coming back.

"You don't have to own a business to make that principal work for you. The *employee* who does more that the boss expects is always going to be successful, because that work ethic is rarely found among workers. *Action* is the key."

When you do <u>more</u> than people expect,
they want to keep you around.

(And they'll <u>reward</u> you to
make sure you stay around.)

That's rather simple, isn't it?

David Carter

I kept the finished logo book in my closet for close to a year. One evening, I was going through all the materials I had collected. It wasn't a pleasant experience. I had sunk a lot of work in my book, and I had formulated a dream — based on the success of the book. For some reason, I began reading the letters of permission that companies had sent to me along with their logos. As I flipped through the pages, my heart began to race. About a third of the letters included a sentence which said something like *"when the book is available, let me know where I can buy a copy."* **BUY** a copy! I was exhilarated. The next morning, I called several short-run book manufacturers to get price quotes on printing a thousand copies of my book. (Low bid was $1,444 for 1,000 copies hardbound.) I immediately sent out letters to everyone who had a logo in the book, offering a special pre-publication price of $7.50, plus $1.00 for shipping (If the prices sound cheap, remember that this was 1972.)

Within three weeks, I had $2,100 in the bank from book sales. I was in the publishing business. And I had *already* made a profit. How did that happen? Simple.

- I listened to a student who wanted a book.
- I listened to a librarian who said "there's nothing like this"
- I listened to myself and said "I want a book like that, too."
- I listened to people who wrote hundreds of letters saying "let me know where I can buy a copy of your book."

But once I had listened, I took **action**.

My wife looked at the pile of 1,000 books and said "what do you plan to do with all those?" I told her I thought all of them would be sold within two years. Once again, I was wrong. They were gone in three months. Another thousand copies were sold in three more months. I was a successful young publisher (I was only 29.) — all because I listened. Before long, I got ideas for other books about logos (mostly from listening).

I often wonder how many other people looked for a logo book, couldn't find it and said ... "*somebody* should do a logo book." I didn't do anything difficult. *Anybody* could have done the book I did. But anybody didn't do it. *I* did. Although I was already free-lancing in the advertising business, my book publishing venture was the beginning of my life as an entrepreneur. I didn't know it then, but it changed my life forever.[1]

[1] I have produced more than 70 books in the field of trademarks and corporate identity. Those books have sold more than a half-million copies.

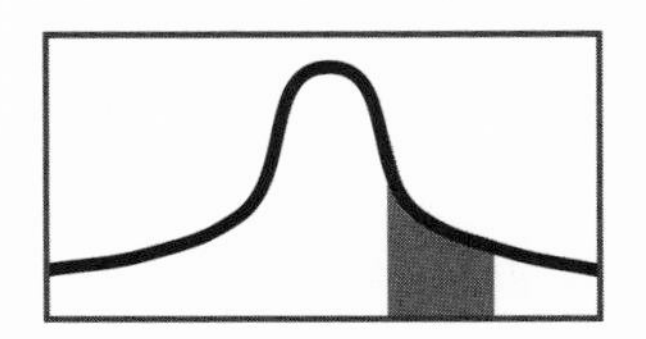

6. Learn to "steal time."

Let's see... the day has 24 hours, and a week has 7 days. That's 168 hours in a week. These are constraints we all have to live with. Unless you're an overachiever. People who reach high levels of success have all learned to find ways to stretch the dimension of time in order to accomplish more. I call this "stealing time." If you're going to really become an overachiever, you'll have to learn how to steal time.

Why stealing time is so important.

Reaching a high level of success is greatly dependent upon *your ability to accumulate knowledge and to develop skills* which relate to your personal goals. For now, let's refer to this body of knowledge and set of skills as "experience." Unfortunately, you cannot pull up to an experience "gas tank," and say "fill it up." Gaining experience takes time. And this is where the ability to steal time becomes so important. If you can "steal" a couple of hours a day (time which your peers are wasting), you're getting a huge jump on your competition — you're gaining the experience you need for success at a much faster rate than they are.

Let's take a typical business, which has just hired two trainees with the same essential educational background and level of intelligence. They start off as equals. But Employee A utilizes the lunch hour as a way to steal time, while Employee B uses lunch for .... well, eating, and maybe a little window-shopping.

Employee A either brown-bags it (healthy food, of course), or perhaps uses the office microwave to fix a casserole (low-cal, or course, with 100% of all the necessary vitamins and minerals). While Employee A has lunch at the desk, (or in a corner of the lunch room) she is using that time to read trade journals, or put extra time and thought into problem solving, or ... you get the idea. Meanwhile, Employee B is having a greasy lunch loaded with calories and cholesterol, then window shopping (probably in a drizzle, and possibly catching a cold.)

If this pattern continues for a year, Employee A will have 2250 hours of "experience," while employee B will have only 2000 (or perhaps less, since she may miss some work due to the ill effects of all that greasy lunch food.)

Food jokes aside, Employee A is going to have acquired 12.5% more "experience" than Employee B, just from using her lunch hour productively.

If you want to really make a giant leap forward in gaining experience, you can steal *another* five hours a week You can steal one hour in the early evening, five days a week. There's a lot of dead time after work and before whatever you do in the evening, so it's a great time to steal one *more* hour each day. If you can steal *two* hours a day — ten hours a week (one hour at lunch, one in the evening), you're now ready to really blow ahead of your possible competitors. "Stealing" just two hours a day is going to work magic on your body of skills and knowledge. While Employee B is gaining 2000 hours of experience each year, you'll get 2500 — a difference of 25%. In one year, Employee B has gained exactly 12 months of experience. By "stealing" 2 hours a day, you'll get the equivalent of 15 months experience in one calendar year.

(For you young singles who are whining and saying "but what about my social life?" My response is this: If you *really* think you need seven hours for a date — instead of six — maybe you bought the wrong book.) Notice that a lot of these hints have the word "read" in them. Reading is one of the best ways to add to your skills and knowledge. There are so many trade journals out there that can help you gain critical knowledge — not to mention specialized business books, the *Wall Street Journal, Business Week*, etc.

If *one year* of "stealing time" can make that much difference, it really becomes significant over a period of several years. The following two charts show the "accumulated skills and knowledge" of three different people. Each started with one "unit of ability." One has grown at a 3% rate per year. Another has a 10% growth rate. The last one — the overachiever — has a "body of knowledge" growth rate of 20% per year. Just look at the results after ten years. (see below).

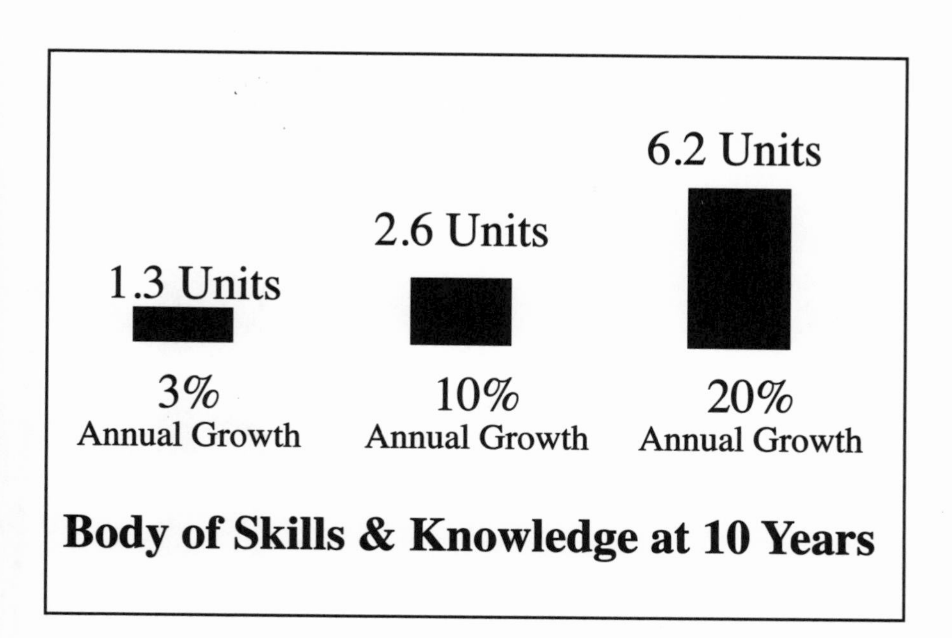

The person who had only a 3% annual growth of "experience" went from one "unit" at the beginning to only 1.3 units after ten years. The person who was acquiring new skills and knowledge at a 10% rate actually doubled that rate to have 2.6 units. But look at the overachiever — her skill and knowledge base grew from one unit to 6.2!

And that's just in the first ten years. When you look at the twenty-year chart, the results are simply astonishing.

The person plodding along at the 3% rate (the typical underachiever) has taken twenty years to go from one unit of skills and knowledge to 1.8 units. The 10% annual growth rate produced a total of 6.7 units. But the overachiever, who maintained the 20% annual rate of growth had gone from one unit to *38.3 units* — more than six times that of the person who had the 10% growth rate. If you compare the overachievers in this book to their "average" peers, you'll see that they're all growing at 20% each year or more.

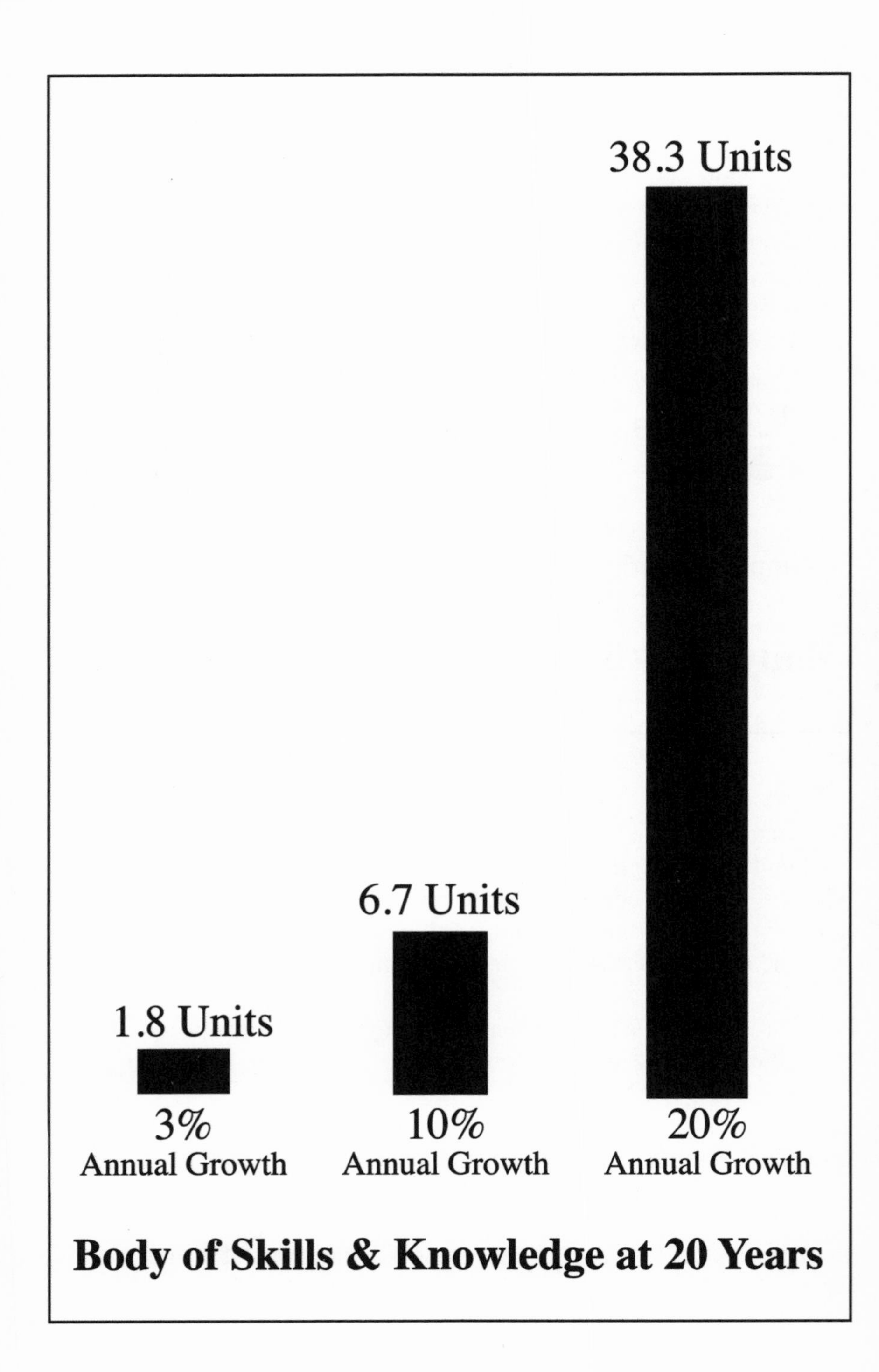
38.3 Units
6.7 Units
1.8 Units
3%
Annual Growth
10%
Annual Growth
20%
Annual Growth
Body of Skills & Knowledge at 20 Years

Jim Harris

Jim Harris has the greatest range (and depth) of knowledge of all the people I know. One day I called to tell him that I was going to Indonesia. "The language there doesn't have any verb tenses," he said. ("How does he know that," I wondered.) Once I visited Jim in California and stayed a few days at his home. I bought a neat new book full of Hollywood trivia — some of it pretty obscure stuff. He saw me reading the book and said "ask me any question in there." I thumbed through it and found a good (tough) question.

"What was Farley Granger's real name?" I asked him. "Jimmy Stewart," he said instantly. "Find something tougher." I looked into the book and got what I thought was a good one. "What did the 'Hollywood sign' originally say?""Hollywood*land*," he said. "It was a real estate development's sign. Don't give me the easy stuff." I went to the back of the book and started reading questions straight down the page. I gave him about twenty tough ones. He got them *all* right. The last one involved an obscure Irish actor. I put the book down, and made some comment about Ireland. He then gave me a 3-minute history of Irish tax laws regarding authors.

Jim reads incessantly, and his personal library has books "double parked" on shelves that fill a room. I guess the message here is that if you want to be a Hollywood producer, *any* kind of knowledge might come in handy. Matter of fact, if you want to be *anything*, reading a wide range of stuff can't hurt.

If we could accurately measure Jim's "annual rate of increase" of his knowledge and skills, I'd guess that the bar would go off the top of the page — by a lot.

David Warren

When David Warren was flying all over the country, he was able to steal quite a bit of time in airplanes. "You can either sleep, eat, talk to the neighbor next to you — or work. I always got an aisle seat and brought work with me. I got a great deal of reading done, or spent the time working. On a coast-to-coast flight, I would steal five hours of time. I'd watch other executives spend four hours watching two movies and think

'I just gained four hours on that guy.' "On short trips to do industrial consulting, I might have a 4 or 5 hour drive each way. I really believe that I got the equivalent of a Ph.D. just from listening to learning cassettes. I bought a lot of the tapes, and I would listen to each one several times in a row. I found that it takes that many repetitions to really get the message. It's like listening to music. After you hear it several times, it becomes part of your memory."

Teresa Wright

Teresa "steals time" by listening to motivational tapes in her car and by "going to the office late at night when I get more done. But I also steal time by the fact that whenever I'm anywhere around people, I'm ready to meet new acquaintances and give them my card.*

"In effect, wherever I go, I'm working, since I'm always ready to meet new prospects."

*Her business card has her photo on it. Once you've met Teresa, you'll never forget her. And if you want to buy or sell a house, there's a good chance you'll want to have her involved.

Randy Carniak

Randy works in New York City, but lives far away in a seaside community. In order to have his lifestyle of choice in a small New Jersey town, he has a two-hour train ride — each way — every day. "I use those four hours just as though I were in my office. I read important articles about business, I analyze reports, I prepare presentations, and the result is that I'm stealing 20 hours a week. Every day, I see many of the same people on the same train doing the same thing — sleeping or reading the paper or playing cards.

"Can you imagine spending 20 hours a week playing cards — just to pass time. If I'm going to have to be on the train that much, I'm going to really use that time to my benefit."

Mal Charles

In the years while he was still working his "regular job," Mal would spend every weekend on the road, selling his creations at flea markets and at carnivals. Before long, carnival operators noticed the quality of his airbrush drawings on T-shirts and asked him to do painting for carnival rides, fun houses, and similar attractions. To meet the demand of that market, he would take vacation days from his job.

"I left one Thursday after work, flew to California that night, and painted a haunted house on Friday and Saturday. I flew home on Sunday and was back on the job Monday morning. I had taken only one vacation day from work. Working a schedule like that made it possible for me to make more money from my "sideline" than I was from my regular job.

"Today, I use machines to steal time. If one machine can produce 40 finished pieces per hour, then I can double or triple that just by adding more machines."

Brad Thomas

"First of all, for a long time I worked 18-hour days. My competition was working 8 or maybe 10 hours. For the first few years, I didn't sleep more than 4 or 5 hours a night. I was in my early twenties then, and I could do that.

"When a customer needed me to be there — no matter what time — I was there. If I got a call at midnight on Sunday, or noon on Sunday, or Christmas eve, I was there. When my competitors would say, 'I can't get to you until next Tuesday,' I'd say, 'I can be there tonight.' I worked most holidays because that's when industrial plants would shut down. My family paid a big price back then, but I worked night and day. Many times, I'd sleep in the truck.

"When we had a job at a big industrial plant near my home, I'd set my alarm clock for two a.m. I'd get up and slip over to the plant, check on my employees for about 30-45 minutes, then go back home and sleep 2-3 more hours before getting up again. I'd be back at the plant by 7. My customers saw that I was really committed to taking care of their needs.

David Carter

I've found a lot of ways to steal time. I discovered long ago that most business lunches are a waste of time, so I microwave a low-cal meal at least four days a week. (Four hours stolen right there.)

I used to have a 30-minute commute (each way) from where I lived to my office. Fourteen years ago, we found a terrific place to live — six acres in the woods, and it's just ten minutes from my office. I cut out 40 minutes a day driving time — that's over 160 hours a year! I "stole" a *month* a year just by moving. (Over a 14-year period, I've "stolen" a year and two months.)

I also use otherwise dead time to do productive things. When my wife and I take short trips out of town, we take turns driving. During her two-hour shift, I read trade journals, or find some other way to make that time productive. I actively look for ways to steal time. It's amazing how much more you can get accomplished when stealing time becomes a way of life for you.

Ten Great ways to steal time

1. Take your computer manuals home with you. (And, of course, read them.) You'll soon know a lot of stuff about your office computer that nobody else knows. *That* knowledge will get you a lot of recognition.

2. Take a *computer* home with you. If you don't have a company-owned laptop, invest in one yourself. It'll impress the heck out of the boss, and you'll really become a highly productive person.

3. While you watch "Wheel of Fortune" and "Jeopardy," read something valuable. (Not the comics.) Don't say that you can't watch TV while you read. You did it in high school, didn't you?

4. When you're driving, listen to a motivational or career-based

tape. One good idea from a tape will do your career more good than listening to 1,000 Howard Stern jokes. (Unless, of course, you want to be a comedy writer.)

5. While you exercise, instead of listening to music tapes, listen to motivational tapes. Or business books on tape. Or a language tape. (Maybe Sony will come out with an "Overachiever Walkman.")

6. When you go to the doctor or dentist, you're going to have some waiting time (it could be significant.) Take along something productive to do. Otherwise, you'll wind up reading a *People* magazine that you may have seen six months ago. (How many articles about Leonardo DiCaprio do you actually need to read?)

7. While you're at the barber or hairdresser, take your own reading material. (Do stories like "I was impregnated by space aliens" really help you reach goals?) At thirty minutes per session, twenty times a year, you can steal ten hours a year this way.

8. Make a written list of things you have to do. By listing all of your pending tasks, you can organize your time better — and even combine some things which will save lots of time. A written list will also make sure you don't forget an important task.

9. Go to the office occasionally on Saturday afternoon — or when no one else is there. You get about twice as much done, because there are no phone calls or interruptions from other people.

10. If you commute to work in heavy traffic, leave early and go home later. Look at is this way: Say you have a 45 minute commute in heavy traffic, (leave at 7:15 to get there at 8:00). If you leave at 7:00 — before the traffic gets bad, your commute is only 25 minutes. You've stolen 20 minutes on the way to work — but it cost you 15 minutes (leaving earlier). Same thing going home. Traffic at 5:00 is awful; you face another 45 minute commute. But if you leave at 5:30, you get home in 25 minutes. What you've done is arrive at the office at 7:25 (not 8:00), and you stay until 5:30, not 5:00. So, you were productive at work for an extra 55 minutes for the day. To steal that 50 minutes, you had to "give up" 15 minutes in the morning (leave at 7:00, not 7:15), and give up 10 minutes in the evening (get home at 5:55, not 5:45). But, by doing that, you've traded 25 minutes more away from home for 50 minutes of extra office productivity. You've stolen over two hours a week — or more than 2 1/2 weeks in a year!

Important note: Most likely, you have found a few ways to steal time which work well for you. If so, write me a note, tell me how you steal time, include your name and address, and you may even see your idea (and your name) in another book I'll be writing soon. Send your idea to David Carter, c/o London Books, Ltd., 4100 Executive Park Dr., #16, Cincinnati, OH 45241.

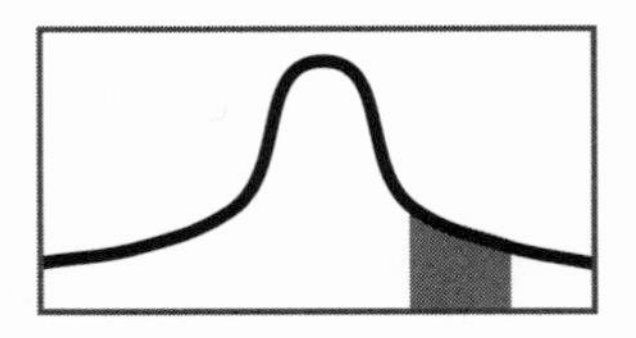

7. Promote yourself.

Once you start to be highly productive, it's important that the *right* people know about it. If you work for a corporation (as opposed to being self-employed), you have to be a little careful about what my grandmother would call "tooting your own horn." For the most part, your outstanding work in a corporation will be noticed by good supervisors. (If you work for a bunch of people who don't recognize excellent work, maybe you'd better start looking around for a new employer, anyway.)

Jim Harris

As a writer in the television industry, Jim Harris had a different set of restraints as he promoted himself.

"At the Carson show, I always tried to turn in at least 12 pages every day. It was important to me that I would have more *quantity* of material turned in than anyone else. But it was equally important that the *quality* of my material was very high. The writers all had an informal 'scorecard' of how many of their jokes made the show each night. It was never written down, but everyone kept count. I always had a high number of jokes which 'made the cut.'"

"As I spent more time in the business, I became more adept at writing really good material — quickly." (*Author's note:* Jim was with the Johnny Carson show — three separate times — for a total of more than 13 years.) "When I went back to the Carson show the last time, I was very experienced, and most of the writing staff was in their late twenties. The first few weeks I was there, I made a big effort to turn in more total material than the rest of the staff *combined.* That made a big impression on a lot of people.

"In my early years in Hollywood, I became known as a writer who would stand up to defend my best work from 'snipers' — people who would want to make changes just for the sake of having some input into the show. One day at a meeting, I reacted rather strongly to a request for a change which I thought was senseless. I was sitting at one end of a large walnut conference table — three other people were seated at the other end. I stood up *in my chair* and spoke the lines I had written, and I said 'you can't change this. It's exactly right for the character— just the way it is.' I then did a big 'belly flop' on the long conference table, slid several feet, and wound up face to face with the guy at the other end of the table. I said 'Do you see how strongly I feel about not changing this?' The guy I was facing was in total shock. His face was chalk white. "Leave it your way,' he said meekly. When I crawled off the table to go back to my chair, I noticed that my belt buckle had left a huge scar in the beautiful wooden conference table. For a long time, people remembered me as the guy who would literally fight to keep good writing from being changed. Anybody with a nice conference table never challenged me again."

David Warren

One of David's goals was to be the number one expert in back injury prevention. He wanted to make it happen overnight, which was, of course, impossible It took him about 10 years to reach that goal. A big part of his getting there came from associating with people who had already established reputations in the physical therapy field. David admits that this was part of his strategy. "I established a faculty of nationally known experts — all of whom were much smarter than I was. The nine other people on the panel were all experts. Just by being on the program with them, made me grow in stature — at least in the eyes of people who counted.

"I also got a lot of positive attention by doing things a little differently Our back seminar panel included an Olympic weight lifter, who actually demonstrated how our techniques were so effective. Imagine that — a world-class weight lifter on the panel with a bunch of health care professionals. But it made a strong point, and it made our seminar well remembered.

Becoming successful is much easier if people perceive you as *already* being successful.

Teresa Wright

Teresa Wright works as one of many sales people for a large real estate brokerage, but she found effective ways to engage in self promotion.

"Just getting a lot of home listings gets your name around," she says, "because the sales person's name and phone number go on the 'for sale' sign in the yard."

She's right. The first time I ever heard of Teresa was when my pre-adolescent daughter was riding home from school with me one day. "How come all the really nice houses that are for sale have Teresa Wright's name on the sign?" she asked. I began to notice that the most expensive homes in town were being sold by one person — Teresa. That's a great reputation to have, and it helped to get Teresa's name well known in the area.

Teresa also has a more pro-active approach to self promotion. As she sat in my office, she said "I try to give out my business card to five people every day. That's 25 cards a week; over a thousand in a year. A lot of those people wind up calling me to buy or sell a house." She had three cards in her hand. As she left, she gave two of the cards to the women who run my office. Two days later, Missy, my office manager, called Teresa to ask about a house that she liked. A few weeks later, Teresa sold the house to my office manager. She came to my office to be interviewed for this book, and she wound up selling a house. No wonder she is so successful.

Randy Carniak

"They tell salesmen that they should 'ask for the order.' I let it be known that I was out to move up in the company. I told my immediate boss, but I also told the company president. I was a little bold back then. I had seen people literally hide their ambitions, hoping that someone would ask them to move up. The problem is — that false modesty is often seen by management as a lack of desire to advance. When I was in my early twenties, I was viewed as a 'gunslinger.' I was very aggressive — sometimes a little too aggressive — but I made it known that I had ambition.

"But beyond that aggressiveness, I took steps which I knew were important to get the attention of the right people. I dressed right. I planned what I would wear each day. After all, I worked for a clothing company. First impressions are so important, and I worked very hard to achieve the 'corporate look.' I dressed like the people that I wanted to work beside someday.

Having the right personal appearance is very important to your success in business. There is a great book titled *Dress for Success* by John Malloy, which I recommend highly. There's also a similar book by Malloy directed toward women. Buy one of these books. It's a small investment in your career that will pay off immediately. People *do* judge you by your appearance.

"Appearance was important to my career plan, but so was substance. When I was going to make a presentation at a meeting, I had one goal: *total* preparation. I wanted to make my presentations so complete that there could be only a few harmless questions. I have seen people who went in unprepared and really hurt themselves by not being ready to respond to any questions. I tried to answer all the possible questions beforehand — in the presentation I made."

You are measured not only by what you do,

but by the *perception* of how you do it.

Mal Charles

"While I was selling T-shirts on the carnival circuit, I had a chance to paint a couple of rides for a fun house. The show and carnival painting business is all word of mouth. If you don't do a good job in New York, they'll know it in California the next week. But its the same way if you make them happy. They'll tell their friends. Carnival operators aren't the guys you see out front — the guys who haven't shaved for three days. When I go to their annual convention in Florida, I see them driving up in their Rolls Royces. The big operators are all successful businessmen ... smart businessmen. And they appreciate good work. I did good work for a few of these people, and they told others about it. They helped spread my reputation."

Brad Thomas

"When I'd go check a job, it was important that I saw my customer's supervisor to let him know how it was going. It was very important to let my customers know that I was on top of things. When I was there on midnight shift, I made sure that the supervisor knew that I was there. I wanted to make sure he'd tell his boss that I was there in the middle of the night.

"You have to get to know the people who can help make you successful, and let them know that you'll do whatever you can to fill their needs.

David Carter

I used my success with logo books to go into advertising full time. When I first started an ad agency, it seemed like my name was in the paper every few weeks. (It was.) Well, I planted most of those stories, and I timed the planting so that it would provide a "harvest" at the right time. Once, I got awards from three different advertising competitions — all in the course of one week. But instead of having one story about my three awards, I wrote three separate news releases, several weeks apart. The impact of those three articles had people saying to me "you're always getting advertising awards." Most important, prospective clients saw those articles, and this helped my business grow. Every time something good (and newsworthy) happened to me or my business, it got in the local paper, because I wrote the news release myself and took it there.

I'll now say in print what I've admitted privately for a long time: I was a shameless self promoter when I was growing my advertising business. But — it was a necessity. (See next page.)

No matter how qualified you might be,

if the right people don't know about it, it doesn't count.

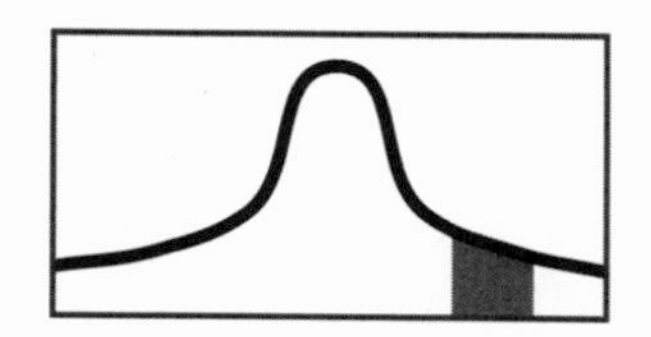

8. Look for ways to "double promote" yourself.

Let me explain what I mean by "double promotion." I use the phrase in the sense of a bright child who finishes fourth grade, and the teacher says "you don't need to waste your time in the fifth grade, we're going to put you in sixth grade this year." In school, double promotion means skipping a grade.

For overachievers, double promotion means that valuable time in not wasted by simply "waiting in line" for time to pass. When you "double promote" yourself, the effect is to leapfrog over people who are ahead you — but are moving at a slower pace. You can get so much further ahead of the pack, since you aren't wasting years simply waiting for something to happen.

The people in this book have found some intriguing ways to double promote themselves.

Jim Harris

"I have one rule. Well, actually, two.

"One, forget conventional wisdom. That's an oxymoron of the first order. There's nothing conventional about wisdom. And two, never take yes for an answer. After I got the Tonight Show goal I had so doggedly pursued, I didn't look upon that as my final destination. I used the Tonight Show job as leverage to sign with New York's largest talent agency — William Morris. This is the same agency that sent my material back un-opened just weeks before. I now held two aces: the Carson

Show and William Morris. That combination opened many doors which either of them separately could not. I did punch-up work for several movies based on (a.) the fact that I was a writer for the Tonight Show, and (b.) I had a major-league agent who could tell the client things like: I was one of Woody Allen's favorites when he would guest host the Tonight Show — and since Woody was a film writer and he liked me, then, by golly, that made me a film writer too.

"I was by no means the most successful at the double promotion game on the Tonight Show staff. One fellow I worked with co-wrote Woody Allen's first two movies while he was still with the Carson show, and another guy used his background as a musician and his Tonight Show position to get a job producing and performing on the *Deliverance* sound track album. The money he made from that allowed him to quit the Tonight Show and take a shot at writing movies full time. He got his first major movie assignment three months later. About two years after that, I watched him pick up an Oscar for Best Original Screenplay."

David Warren

The single most important step for David was coming out of school and working for a P.T. who was a highly regarded individual, but who was also his "mentor."

Although David was just out of school, he saw the importance of working under the right role model. "Before I graduated, I found out about a brilliant physical therapist and arranged for a 3-week study with him. I got enormously excited about my career opportunities, because he was brilliant clinically, he was very bright, and extremely motivated. He read a lot, and he took a lot of continuing education courses. I knew if I came to work for him, it would literally catapult my career. In one or two years with him, I could advance far beyond any of my classmates. I felt that by learning from my mentor, I would soon be five to ten years ahead of my peers. After I graduated, I struck a deal with the therapist that I would come and work with him as long as he would allow me unlimited continuing education. This would allow me to take every course available that pertained to our field. I wanted to learn how to take care of back patients, and he gave me the time off work to attend those classes. After two years, I had taken every course available on the treatment of back injuries. I was still in my mid-twenties, but I was a back injury expert."

Teresa Wright

Since her income is based on sales commissions, Teresa had no ceiling on her income — nor did she have a floor. Her success was totally dependent upon her ability to sell.

Teresa is not content to sit, be part of the pack, and wait for things to happen. In order to attract new listings and make sales faster, she has her own real estate ad in the newspaper — separate from that of the successful agency which employs her. That's a perfect example of "double promotion."

While Teresa has found many ways to quickly advance her career and skip rungs on the ladder, she's quick to note that "hard work is the key element — because so many people simply won't make that commitment.

"And, I never forget my past clients. I keep in touch with them, and they appreciate it. People move, on average, every seven years. I get a lot of repeat business."

Randy Carniak.

When I looked at Randy's 2-page resume, I was astounded. First of all, he's only 35 years old, and is national sales manger for a large, nationally-known corporation. But the really amazing part is that *he has never been a salesman on the road.*

The typical national sales manager has "paid his dues" with a number of hard years on the road, followed by several more years as district or regional sales manager. The typical time needed to advance from a road sales position to "national sales manager" is anywhere from 10 to 25 years. *Randy bypassed this part altogether.*

"After I had gained a lot of experience in managing people in marketing, I did my best to let the company president know that managing sales people was no different than managing marketing people. And — while I was marketing manager, I spent a lot of time with the road salesmen in order to learn all I could about their job. In the end, it became obvious that I really didn't need to have been a road salesman in order to properly manage the whole sales staff.

Mal Charles

"I double promoted myself by becoming a businessman. I skipped from carnivals and flea markets to a location in a huge mall. People who were buying from me at flea markets were no different from mall customers. It's all about finding out what people want. You have to fill their desires — at their price. That means you have to work fast. There are literally thousands of artists working flea markets, and most of them do really good work. I certainly wasn't the best airbrush artist working the circuit. But in order to do really big volume, you have to have a store — like my mall location. The problem with that is — you have to become a businessman. Most 'art people' never take that huge step. They're content to do whatever design they like and hope it will sell. I wasn't the best artist out there — I was just the one with the courage to open a store in a mall.

"Becoming a businessman — thinking like a businessman — opened up a whole new world for me. Otherwise, I'd still be working flea markets and carnivals on weekends."

Brad Thomas

"We grew at a rate of over 100% per year, even up to the $15 million mark. The difficult part in doing that wasn't in getting the contracts, but in getting the *people* to help make the business succeed. The company was able to grow so fast because I attracted people who wanted to be a part of what I was building.

"If I had been content with growth of even 20% a year, for example, I would have never reached the five million dollar mark. But with our growth rate, I was almost at $50 million when I sold the company."

David Carter

I've skipped a lot of steps on a lot of ladders. And occasionally, I've even decided to change ladders.

In 1978, I was asked by *Advertising Age* magazine to conduct three seminars on corporate identity — in New York, Chicago and Los Angeles. At that time, I had written about ten books about logos, and had created maybe 50 logo designs for mostly small firms.

I saw the seminars as a way to help me move up the ladder quickly. I realized that I would never be competitive with the big-name corporate identity consultants. My Kentucky location was going to be a negative factor if I even attempted to do that. But I was very interested in doing work internationally.

A normal strategy would be:

1. Become well known regionally (5 years)
2. Become well known nationally (10 years)
3. Enter the international market (3 years)

I knew that I could never get the large national projects that would let me reach step number two. Yet, I wanted very much to reach step three. So, I formulated a plan that would let me simply *skip over* step two and enter the international market as a logo design consultant.

The plan worked. While I could never get the huge logo projects such as FedEx or BankOne or GE, (because I was "the guy from Kentucky who does logo books"), I've been quite successful in the Asian market. (To people in New York, I'm the guy from down south somewhere, but to businessmen in Asia, I'm the *American.*)

Actually, in Asia, my books served to promote my consulting activities. Since the Asian culture places a high value on education, people who write books are held in high esteem. The books simply proved that I was qualified to be a consultant on corporate identity to big firms there.

Why go 35 miles an hour, when you're capable of doing 140? Get in the passing lane.

On the highway of success, there's no speed limit.

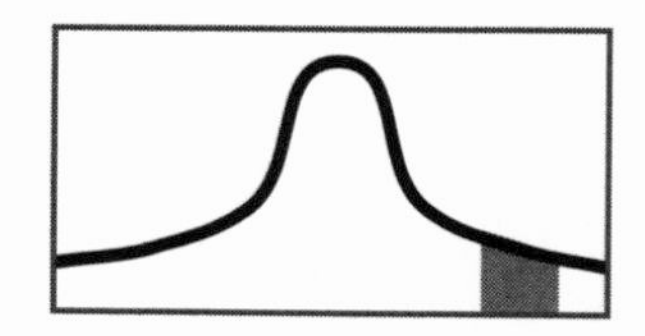

9. Multiply.

I want you to meet four people with stories I think you will find interesting. Here's a quick paragraph about each.

• Dwayne dropped out of high school midway through his senior year and enlisted in the army. After surviving Viet Nam intact, he used the G.I. bill to go to college. Surprisingly, he did very well and became a CPA. By 1990, he was a valued executive with a large firm, making nearly $100,000 a year.

• Lester was from a middle-class family, and could have gone into the business his father had founded. Instead, he chose to make it "on his own." He started as a bank teller, and worked his way up to the presidency of a mid-sized bank by the time he was 40. He was clearly a young achiever. (His father sold the family business and took early retirement.)

• Simon had worked hard to become one of the top three executives in a management consulting firm with more than 200 professional employees. When the chairman decided to retire, Simon had a 50-50 chance of getting the job — at age 45. He would be "set for life" if he became chairman.

•Walter had managed to get several "need-based" scholarships to attend college, and he was able to graduate from one of the nation's most prestigious universities. His career track had some blemishes, as he was fired twice from sales management positions. However, he was able to minimize the damage from those situations, explaining that there were "personality conflicts" involved both times. By age 52, he had reached a major pinnacle of success — he was chosen as president of a growing public company, and his salary was more than $250,000 per year.

These four people had some pretty impressive credentials, but all these "high achievers" became victims of the new economic order.

• Dwayne's firm was one of the early proponents of "corporate downsizing," and he was bright enough to see what was coming. He was certain that his job would be "outsourced," so he began job hunting. He was able to find a job with good long-term security — but at a substantial pay cut. His $95,000 salary fell to $55,000 — but he was happy to still have a job. Two months after he left, his entire department at his old employer was eliminated.

• Lester's bank was involved in a "friendly" merger, but the composition of the board of directors soon changed. Lester was no longer favored to lead the bank; he was given a one-year severance pay. However, as his generous settlement was running out, Lester still couldn't find a suitable job, as the number of banks in the U.S. was shrinking rapidly. Eventually, Lester settled for a job outside the banking industry making 40% of his old salary. His wife went back to work for the first time in twenty years.

• Simon really thought that he had a good chance to succeed the retiring chairman. But so did the *other* top executive — who became Simon's adversary. The outgoing chairman put the job up for grabs with a 3-month "contest," which became vicious and competitive. When Simon's rival was chosen for the job, he didn't take any chances on having a disgruntled executive around — Simon was immediately fired. After looking for the right situation for seven months, Simon invested his life's savings in buying half interest in a small consulting firm.

•Walter's board of directors knew that a recession was going on, but they expected that the annual earnings report would show more profits than Walter had produced. The board decided that someone else could run the company better than Walter. He was fired without warning, and his $250,000 per year salary turned to vapor. Walter's *third* firing seemed to make him into an "untouchable" in the business world. He was unemployed for more than two years, and finally took a position as sales manager of a small firm. He had last been a lowly sales manager" twenty years ago.

All these people have a common bond. Each was a very high achiever, and each was on a fast career track. But each also discovered just how treacherous life is when a high income can be taken away by a decision made by somebody else. The recent "downsizing of corporate America" has turned hundreds of thousands of former high achievers into unemployed (or under-employed) people who live in fear for their futures.

This narrative would not have been needed just a few years ago. Back then, qualified executives could find a new job quickly. However, the realities of corporate life in America today are harsh. The big salary is a two-edged sword. The sad fact is that millions of highly qualified people have become casualties of the new economic order. Once upon a time[1] the big firms offered "security." Today, the executive suites in America are filled with people who wonder "will the next cut-back get *me*?"

True overachievers don't have this concern because they discover the magic of multiplication. When you learn to *multiply* your success, you really join the rank of overachievers. And best of all, multiplying your efforts gives you a freedom that few people will ever know.

The overachiever definition of multiplication

means having several different sources of income.

You aren't just locked into one venture (or one paycheck) — and if any single part of your efforts has problems, you have the other sources of income in place to soften the potential loss. And surprisingly, people with several sources of income often work *fewer* hours — not more — than when they had only one business interest.

Right now, you're probably concerned only with getting to the first step — reaching that high level of achievement. But you can learn a lot from how our cast of overachievers has multiplied their efforts — and their incomes.

[1] "Once upon a time" may sound like the beginning of a fairy tale. But in this story, the big bad wolf is often the corporation. And this fable does not often have a happy ending.

Jim Harris

When Johnny Carson retired from the Tonight Show in 1992, Jay Leno asked Jim to stay on as a monologue writer. He did, for two years, on the condition that he be allowed to work on other shows at the same time.

Though Jim had a high reputation as talk show writer, he realized that the business had changed. Sitcoms (situations comedies) were now king. He used the early months of the Leno show as an opportunity to branch out into sitcoms full time. Jim had been given many opportunities to work on situation comedy staffs through the years, but he preferred to stay with Johnny Carson.

But now Carson had retired, and Jim had to ask himself "what do I want to do next?" He knew that sitcoms were the direction to take, but he wanted to be involved as a writer-producer, not just as a writer.

It normally takes five to seven hard years of work to move up to the senior producer levels in the sitcom world. Jim had no interest in going that route. He quickly wrote two spec scripts. (A spec script is one which is *not* assigned by the show for which it is written, but is created by a writer hoping he can impress someone enough for them to assign a script in the future. These scripts are seldom read, much less purchased and produced.)

Due to Jim's reputation and credentials, the scripts were read and both of them were purchased *and* produced. Many others in Jim's profession thought they were "above" writing a spec script. Even at that point in his career, with more than 20 years as a highly successful writer, Jim was still willing to bet on himself. Except this time he used his Tonight Show reputation and resume to start a career in sitcoms at a very high level. Then, once there, he stayed long hours and sat in on production meetings, showing that he had the ability to move into executive production levels.

The end result was that Jim was given the chance to multiply his opportunities. He has learned to multiply very well. As this is written, he is working on three different network TV shows (all in the Nielsen top 12), as well as creating a pilot for a fourth show (A fifth is in the planning stages.) And, Jim is set to receive money in the mail as each of these shows goes into syndication.

David Warren

David has learned to multiply several times. When he was doing his back school programs, he sold publications, slide programs, and videos. All of these were ways to make money without any personal time involvement. There's a certain magic to getting "money in the mail" that allows overachievers to multiply their income while also multiplying their leisure time.

David sold his back school several years ago in order to concentrate on building a chain of physical therapy clinics. Now, with three locations for his PT centers, he plans to expand rapidly in the next few years.

"The first one is the tough one," he said. "But once you know the market and the process, it's a matter of good planning. And my long range goal is to work very hard to get everything up and running, then I'll have people working for me — managing what I've created."

Teresa Wright

It's difficult to multiply when you're an individual real estate sales person. But Teresa Wright did it. "I just took in a real estate partner. I was too busy, so I looked for a long time until I found someone whose abilities match with mine. My strong point is "lassoing" prospects. His is in details. We share income 50-50, so that forces me to work smarter, not harder. By using a team concept, we're both more productive, and we've been able to accomplish things I could never have done alone. We both produce income for each other — and we're each making more than either of us could alone.

Randy Carniak

While I was interviewing Randy, he looked over my list of overachievers and said "I don't think I belong in this book."

For the first eight chapters, Randy seemed to be a good fit with the rest of the people. He's in a very responsible position for his age, he supervises 14 people, and he has a bright future.

But Randy was right. He's not an overachiever — yet. He's a very high achiever, and is most likely on his way to becoming an overachiever. But Randy has one constraint that no one else in this book has: Randy works for someone, and as a result, he has a "salary cap.[1]" His income is limited to the amount that his boss decides to pay him. Everyone else featured in this book has the ability to make a decision to earn additional money, and then do things to make it happen. Randy can't do that yet.

Randy is on a payroll, therefore he doesn't have the ability to multiply. Only a very few people who collect a regular paycheck (signed by someone else) qualify as overachievers. (Sales people with commission-based income are a notable exception.) But for the large majority of high achievers who work for someone else, the term "overachiever" will never apply to them — because they can't multiply.

Remember the high achievers from the beginning of this chapter? All of them were on top of the world one day — and unemployed the next. For people who made more than $100,000 a year in their old job, finding a new position at a similar salary can take up to a year — or longer. The job market isn't what it used to be. And it may never be that good again.

[1]Randy will appear in my forthcoming book "How to Remove Your Salary Cap" (Subtitle: How to start your own business, without leaving your day job — yet.)

Mal Charles

Mal Charles is just 37 years old, but he's learning the magic of multiplication. His original mall store has expanded significantly in size. During our original interviews for this book, he talked about planning for additional locations. Looking to the future, he was in the early stages of designing a program which will let him franchise his business.

But as this book went to press, Mal had left his mall location, with its high traffic count and its high rents. He had "downsized" and was running a business that catered to corporate customers — providing custom embroidered apparel. He had discovered that he needed to change in order to remain competitive — and happy.

Brad Thomas

Brad may have dropped out of college, but he is a master of multiplication. Once his first business venture was fairly successful, he started a second company, then a third, then a fourth. In order to make them more attractive to a potential corporate merger, he adopted a common "umbrella" name as an identifier for the four businesses.

And when he sold his company for $23 million, he wasn't content to sit and "clip coupons" to collect interest on bonds. Brad looked over a number of opportunities before he bought a bankrupt sewing factory. Within 18 months, he had turned it into a major money maker. For Brad Thomas, his ability to multiply is like a Midas touch.

David Carter

The first logo book was the start of my entrepreneurial life, but it started as a "sideline" business. Where some people might have done two or three books and then stooped, I kept at it, constantly looking for new angles. I was able to sense ideas that people wanted to know more about, and I did books on those concepts. (My publisher says that I've done more books on logo design than anyone else in the world — more than seventy.)

But as successful as the logo books have been, I still realized the power of multiplication. I used the logo books as a springboard to:

- logo design seminars
- logo design consulting (internationally)
- logo design software
- logo design annual (showing the best new designs)
- being an expert witness in trademark legal cases
- being a source on logo design articles for *USA Today*

Three of the four businesses I own are directly related to designing logos. And the fourth is indirectly related — and it couldn't have happened if I hadn't been doing the logo books.

There's magic in multiplying yourself.

The financial rewards also multiply, but when you get to a certain point, the rewards are really valuable: freedom to leave the office for weeks at a time, and leisure time to do fun things with your family. Those are the best rewards of learning how to multiply.

Money in the Mail

is the Ultimate Reward

for Learning to Multiply Really Well

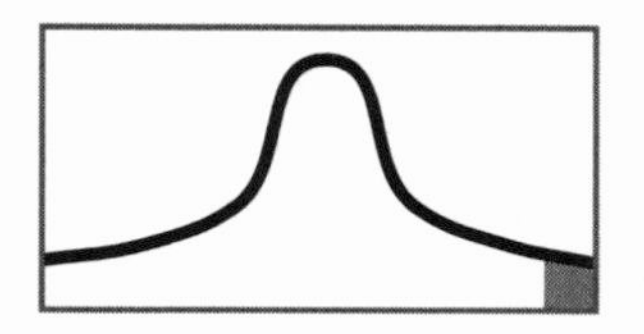

10. "Now, what else can I do?"

(This is so easy, I want to do some more interesting stuff.)

Another thing which sets overachievers apart from the masses is the continual quest for new and interesting things to do. All the people in this book have reached exceptionally high levels of accomplishment. Yet, every one of them has a common feeling: "you ain't seen nothing yet."

Once you reach a certain level of achievement, you'll see that the competition is minimal (because most people are spectators), and you'll also have learned how to spot new opportunities. In addition, the contacts that overachievers make in their journey of success means that many new and interesting doors are easily opened. Often, this process means that the overachiever grows into new areas of interest and finds more major opportunities as a result.

Jim Harris

Most people would look at Jim Harris and say "he has it made." But few people realize the real key to his continuing success. "I still do all the things I was doing when I was trying to make my name known. I read a lot of things — so I can keep getting fresh ideas. And most of all, I listen. It's amazing how many ideas I get just from hearing people talk. And while I'm listed as "producer" [or some variation of that title] on the show credits, I still write a lot. It's important to me that I still get to

create, even though my title would indicate otherwise.
"One of the things that I do outside of my normal routine is write material for politicians. I still have a keen interest in public affairs, and I've written for just about every democrat who didn't become president in the past 20 years."

> Author's note: Jim is being modest here. He's actually provided material for three presidents.

"I have met a lot of people over the years, and there are so many contacts that are important in this business. The ironic thing is that I can pick up a phone and get through to so many important people now. I'm maybe 20% better at what I do now than when I started. But now, it's 1000% easier to make a contact than it was then. The very act of reaching a certain level in this business makes it that much easier to do even more. The political contacts I've made have opened a lot of doors for me."

> Another author's note: Jim denies that he got to sleep in the Lincoln bedroom but I'm not so sure.

You may remember that Jim's early interests involved politics. Now that he has reached a pinnacle of success in Hollywood, he's able to use his writing skills as an entrée to working with some of the best known names in politics.

The more successful you get,

the easier it is to get even *more* success.

David Warren

"Success does become easier as you go along. Experience is a wonderful teacher. I've learned how to cut the learning curve for training new people that I hire. A big part of our growth plan is dependent upon the effecting grooming of new therapists. And for new locations, I've already done the hard part. Now I know how to open a new clinic. I know the square footage needed for a clinic facility, I know what's needed for new equipment, and I know how to evaluate a new market area."

Clearly, David Warren learned from his experiences, and he has multiplied his successes. Most successful people will agree that once you have an important body of knowledge, you can really use that as a springboard to other fields. Remember how David used his knowledge of back injuries to begin a successful "back school." When he grew tired of that, he sold it, then began a chain of physical therapy clinics. All the time, he is making new contacts and listening for new ideas. He's in the healthcare field, and many opportunities will be open to him — so you can be sure that he'll be listening for ideas for his next venture.

"Health care is a growth market. There will be a lot of opportunities in the future. You can be sure I'll take advantage of some of those opportunities."

> If David has simply followed the course of most clinical physical therapists, he would still be a clinical physical therapist. But his business experience gives him the potential for many ventures inside the health care field.

Teresa Wright

Recently, Teresa made a big move upward. For most of her career, she had depended upon getting individual listings and selling single-family homes. Now, she has exclusive rights to sell building lots in a private golf course community. There are literally hundreds of lots which she can market. And — if someone else happens to sell any of them, she still gets a part of the commission. She's now poised to *really* multiply her income. And because she now has experience in selling this type of development, she's in a good position to do it again and again. Each step she takes opens new possibilities for her.

Randy Carniak

Randy — our *aspiring* overachiever — realizes that he is limited as long as he works on a payroll. "I know that I have the ability to run a company. I've seen good managers do it; I've been part of the process. But — like this book mentions in the early chapters, I'm still in my comfort zone. I know that if I'm ever going to really be like the other people in this book, I'm going to have to leave my comfort zone, face a little risk, and see how good I really am."

Randy has been preparing himself for the next step. He is involved in continual learning, and he's listening for the voice of opportunity.

"I've done very well so far, but very soon, I'll have to ask myself if I'm r*eally* an overachiever — or just another high achiever."

Brad Thomas

"When I sold the company, I was 39 years old. For twenty years, I had built a business. But with the sale, I had a 5-year agreement to stay on and manage the division, and I took that commitment seriously. The best thing for me was that my job description changed 100% when I sold out. My job was to find and acquire businesses to help the company expand.

"All the learning I had done in those 20 years had given me a good education. That was my 'college.' When I sold my company, I was starting to school again — working for a huge public company was like getting an MBA. Just learning from all the people within a $10 billion company has taught me a lot. It's kept me fresh and interested. I had to go from being an entrepreneur to being a professional manager.

> Most people would have taken the money and walked away. Brad saw his situation as an opportunity to learn from people who were running a multi-billion dollar business. As a result, he has made business and personal contacts that would never have been possible if he had simply "retired."

"It took a tremendous amount of personal growing on my part to make this transition. For the first time in my life, I had bosses to report to. But I'm a firm believer in learning something new every day. Just because I quit college — that didn't mean I quit learning.

"Actually, selling the company was the beginning of a new life for me. I bought a bankrupt shirt factory, and turned it into a moneymaker within 18 months. And I'm actively looking for more things to do. But it's important that I do something I enjoy. If I can't have fun at this stage of my life, why bother?"

For Brad, deciding "what's next?" means having a lot of options. When he sold his business, he received most of the sale price in stock, with a small percent coming as cash. But with a "paper" net worth well into the millions of dollars, he can easily raise the money for just about any investment he wants to make.

At age 44, he's in the position of having a lot of business opportunities come his way. Now, he has the luxury of picking exactly what he wants to do with his money — and his time. That's one of the rewards of becoming a *real* overachiever.

Mal Charles

"The biggest transition in changing from artist to businessman involved the people I deal with. When I was selling my artwork on T-shirts at flea markets, my associates were doing the same thing. Now, as we go to conventions and to visit other stores in the same business we're in, I always pick up buiness-related ideas. I meet an interesting cross-section of business people. When I do that, I see so many possibilities — we're definitely not where we want to be yet. We're refining what we're doing. Success is easy. It happens before you know it. Suddenly, you look back and see that you've done quite a lot. But managing change is what running a business is all about. I just have to have my eyes and ears open so I can make change happen — on my terms."

As this book went to press, Mal had made a change. He closed his mall store, as he found that being in the wholesale business —producing embroideried items to corporate customers — was a stronger business segment to be in. He discovered that "nothing lasts forever." However, for overachievers, the ability to make changes in response to new business conditions is a necessary part of thriving in business.

David Carter

Success *does* get easier as you go along. Part of that is due to the relationships that can be established. Once you have a network of high-level business contacts, many new opportunities suddenly appear. For example, I was doing a seminar in New York City several years ago, and met an entrepreneur from Indonesia. He asked me to bring my seminar to Jakarta. That led to our working together on a single project. Today, we've involved in several joint ventures together. Every time you open one door, it seems like a dozen more new doors appear.

Even though I think globally, I'm still doing the basic things that were important when I started my first business.. I still read lot. And I'm always listening for people to tell me how to succeed. The current buzzword is "lifetime learning." I recently finished the 3-year OPM program (for company owners and presidents) at the Harvard Business School. Why? Because I want to be confident of my ability to identify and profit from new opportunities. If I'm going to compete, I want to win. I believe that the most important thing someone can have in business is **the confidence to change**.

Once they "make it,"

overachievers have a limitless

variety of choices and opportunities.

Making this book work for you.

Now that you've seen how easy "success" is, you're ready to do something with *your* life.

- Start looking for ways to get out of your comfort zone.
- Start listening to people who will tell you to succeed.
- Set some goals for yourself.
- Get ready for that action step.

Don't listen to the negative thoughts of people around you. People will be able to find a thousand reasons why you *can't* reach your goals. You've just read about seven people who did meet their goals. You can do it too.

Nothing's easy. But it can be done. Decide what you want to be, set your goals, and start achieving those goals. Action is the key. *Do it.*

Finally, take time to look up from your day-to-day routine. Frequently ask yourself: "Just how high can I go?"

Remember, people who don't make use of their abilities

are no better off than people who have *no* abilities.

Now — *do something.* And once you've done it, drop a note to me (in care of the publisher). Let me know what you've done, and how this book helped.

Good luck[1]

[1]See the definition of luck on page 57.

Who's Who of Overachievers

Harland Sanders had a very average life until he founded Kentucky Fried Chicken — at age 65.

General Colin Powell was only an average student in college.

Ted Turner partied his way out of Brown University, and never finished college.

Wayne Huizenga dropped out of Calvin College after one year. Ten years later, he founded Waste Management, Inc.

Pete Wilson (U.S. Senator; Governor of California) , failed the bar exam three times before finally passing.

J.P. Morgan worked for his father until he was 50.

Ray Kroc, a mildly successful milk shake machine salesman, started a new business at age 52. (You may have eaten one of his hamburgers. The restaurant chain he founded — McDonald's — has sold more than 100 billion of them.)